For Page
Hope you enjoy this as much as [?] did
with it!

11/10/93

BLUE HORIZONS

Faces and Places
From a Bicycle Journey
Along the Blue Ridge Parkway

Jerry Bledsoe

With photographs by the author

ISBN No. 1-878086-05-7

Library of Congress Catalog Card Number
LC 93-071245

Printed in the United States of America

Cover Design: Harry Blair
Book design: Elizabeth House

Down Home Press
P.O. Box 4126
Asheboro, N.C. 27204

THE BLUE RIDGE PARKWAY

From Rockfish Gap (near Waynesboro, Virginia) to the Oconaluftee Visitor Center (near Cherokee, North Carolina), the Blue Ridge Parkway spans 470.2 miles through six mountain ranges in Virginia and North Carolina.

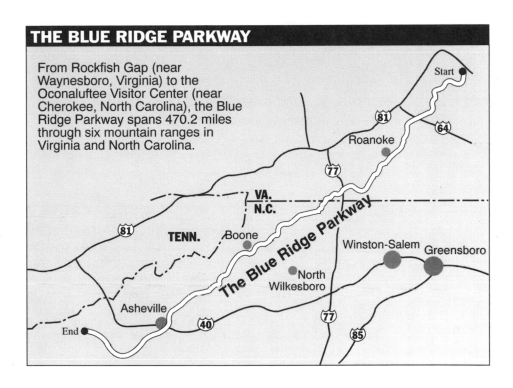

FOREWORD

There are times when it beckons and I must obey.

Often this is in early spring when the trees are blushing at their bareness, or a few weeks later, when the dogwoods have faded and the rhododendron have begun to festoon the roadside in white, pink and lavender, and the flame azaleas are glowing yellow and orange.

Sometimes it is in summer when the lowlands are in a heat-stunned stupor, the high forests are at their lushest, and the distant mountains, cool and haughty, seem a hazy blue dream.

Almost always it summons me in autumn when it is most crowded and at its showiest, dressed in pheasant colors, the air crackly cool, perfumed with apple nectar.

Rarely does it call in winter, for I am not a winter person. Then it can be treacherous – and some would say at its brittle and sparkling best.

Yet in winter it has provided some of my most memorable experiences. One January day, when its surface was slick with ice spots and I was creeping, morosely alone, through fog to the peak of Apple Orchard Mountain in Virginia, I was startled to a full stop by three deer, a young buck and two does, standing smack in the middle of the road. They looked at me as if in wonder that a human should be in such a place at such a time, then ambled off, looking back over their shoulders as if asking themselves, "What on earth could he be doing up here?"

Whatever the season, when the Blue Ridge Parkway beckons me to its comforting bosom, I can't resist. It envelops. It soothes. It stimulates the soul and connects to presences beyond.

A fellow I know once told me that he can find complete peace in only two places on earth: diving a reef at ocean's bottom and sitting on a rock along the Blue Ridge Parkway contemplating the vistas, both inward and outward.

I've been both places and experienced the same feelings, but given my choice, I'd always take the parkway.

People grapple for words in attempting to describe this magnificent highway. Usually they fall back on old reliables such as "spectacular," "beautiful," "restful," "awe-inspiring," "serene."

Not even the Society of American Travel Writers could come up with something original. They voted it the most beautiful highway in America. I agree, but I would go them one better. It may well be the most beautiful highway on earth. Certainly it is one of the most beautiful.

People who know the highway best, those who live along it or have worked on it for years, will tell you that it is never the same. A road of many moods, they say. No matter how many times you travel it, you always encounter something you've never noticed before. It is capricious and rife with surprises.

It is, of course, a national park, a long and slender one to be sure. At points, it is only 200 feet wide. The average width is but 1,000 feet. Its 470-mile length covers only 76,427 acres.

It is a rarity among highways, designed strictly for pleasure and not for utility, a recreational road, haven for picnickers, campers, hikers, bicycle riders, a gentle and welcoming road that serves up memorable views and encourages leisurely driving with frequent stops.

Beginning at Rockfish Gap, just east of Waynesboro, Virginia., the parkway wanders along the crest of six mountain ranges – the Blue Ridge, Black, Great Craggies, Pisgah, Balsams and Great Smokies – at an average elevation of 3,000 feet. At its lowest point, at the James River, north of Lynchburg, Virginia, it is but 655 feet above sea level. At the highest point, in the Great Balsams, south of Waynesville, North Carolina, it rises to 6,050 feet.

The parkway connects two states, Virginia and North Carolina, and two national parks, the Shenandoah and the Great Smoky Mountains. Along the way it passes through 29 counties, skirts two cities, Roanoke and Asheville, crosses five rivers (the James, Roanoke, Linville, Swannanoa and French Broad), traverses four National Forests (George Washington, Jefferson, Pisgah and Nantahala) and slices through the edge of the Qualla Reservation of the Eastern Band of Cherokees before ending at the Oconaluftee River just north of Cherokee.

Enter it at any point and you are apt to feel that you have passed into a garden, as indeed you have, perhaps the most spectacular natural garden in existence, for the mountains that encompass it are called by Encyclopedia Britannica "one of the great floral provinces of earth." Here are to be found more than 2,000 species of plants, a tenth of which grow in no other place. The vast forests through which the parkway passes harbor 140 species of trees and are described by Britannica as "the best and most extensive broadleaf deciduous forests on earth." More than 100 species of birds can be seen along the parkway.

Little wonder then that the parkway is the nation's second most popular national park (just behind Golden Gate National Recreational area, which encompasses the Golden Gate Bridge) and that it records more than 22 million visits each year. Little wonder, too, that it beckons me so frequently and makes me feel so much at home.

CONTENTS

THE DREAM

I don't know where the idea came from, this joining of bicycle and the Blue Ridge Parkway. I only know that it took hold and wouldn't let go. And at some point during the dreariness and hopelessness of a deep winter day, when spring had seemed a promise unlikely to be kept, I affirmed it.

I would do it. If warmth and sunshine ever returned, I would ride my bicycle the entire distance of the Blue Ridge Parkway.

This was a rash commitment for several reasons.

For one, I never had even driven the entire length of the parkway. Although I had paid visits to the parkway almost every year for decades, these usually had been leisurely rituals of spring and fall, homages along the same familiar paths. I didn't even know exactly how long the parkway was. And there were sections of it that I'd never seen, including some that passed over the higher mountains along its route.

When I mentioned my plan to friends and family, some smiled knowingly and let it drop, certain that it was a passing fantasy, the dream of a man trying desperately to cling to the last fading flickers of youth. Others were not so circumspect.

"You're crazy," my friend Greta Tilley told me bluntly. "You're almost 50 years old. You'll have a heart attack and die. It's suicide."

I had to admit that she could be right after I rolled my bike out of the garage on a mild, sunny afternoon in late January and set off on my first ride since late summer. Only four miles from home, struggling up a long, gradual incline, I was forced to stop to catch my breath. My legs trembled. I couldn't believe that I had allowed myself to get so badly out of condition.

A few years earlier, prodded by the first twinges of middle age that I'd allowed myself to acknowledge, overcome by the physical fitness craze that was sweeping the country, I had taken up swimming leisurely laps at the YMCA pool. A Y trainer had convinced me that I also needed to do something for strength, and I soon found myself grunting and straining on Nautilus machines.

After watching me swim, another Y trainer had told me solemnly that it wasn't really doing much for my heart and lungs. What I needed was to sign up for aerobics classes. Next thing I knew, I was hopping awkwardly to rock music in the company of sweaty strangers. The closeness and closed-in-ness of aerobics (not to mention the aromas) had led me at the advent of spring to the openness (and more appealing fragrances) of the outdoors, where I took up jogging in luminous shoes that were ridiculously overpriced. This I had continued rather religiously, usually jogging four miles three times a week, through several pairs of ever brighter and higher priced shoes until the previous summer when joint pains had caused me to question whether jogging might be doing me as much harm as good.

"You need to get a bicycle," another friend, Harry Blair, had told me. "You'll get the same exercise and it won't be as hard on your knees and hips and feet."

I had loved bicycle riding as a kid. I had gotten my first bike, a bright red J.C. Higgins, for Christmas when I was 10, and that and a later bike with chrome fenders had been my primary means of transportation until I was almost 17. My bicycles had given me a great sense of freedom, and there had been few feelings to match that which came on a long downhill run, the wind roaring in my ears as the bike gathered more and more speed.

But I hadn't been on a bike in more than 30 years. And I couldn't remember when I had last seen a bike that looked like the ones I had ridden in my youth. It was true that I had been seeing more and more adults riding bikes in recent years, but the bikes on which they were riding seemed designed more as instruments of torture than as vessels of fun.

These bikes had narrow, delicate tires that didn't look to be sturdy enough to carry an adult. If you hit so much as a pebble with one of those tires you'd expect to go right over the handlebars, which was all the more likely because the handlebars were somewhere south of the wheel spokes. And the seats! They seemed built more for impaling than for offering support and comfort. The riders I saw on these bikes appeared to be grimly attempting to drive themselves into the pavement. And after looking at those brilliantly colored, shiny, skin-tight shorts they all wore, I thought that I understood why. Surely some law must have been passed requiring any adult who got on a bike to wear those shorts. Otherwise, why would anybody spend so much time and energy wriggling in and out of them? For some people I'd seen wearing them, that must have required hours.

"I don't believe I could get hunched over enough to ride a bicycle nowadays," I had told Harry. "Besides, I don't think that I could go out in public in those little tight shorts."

"You don't have to ride like that," he had said. "You can get a mountain bike."

I had never heard of a mountain bike, and Harry explained that it was similar to the bikes we had ridden as kids, with wide knobby tires, a seat broad enough for the body part it was supposed to accommodate and handlebars that curved toward the sky and allowed the rider to sit erect. The big difference was that a mountain bike had a multitude of gears and was rugged enough to travel over rough terrain.

And I didn't even have to put on any of those funny little pants, Harry had assured me while admitting that he did wear them. Those pants were more than just fashionable, he explained. They contained padding that protected against the abrasiveness of bike riding on certain parts of the anatomy.

"You can get a jelly seat," he said.

"A jelly seat?"

"Yeah, it's soft and flexible, feels like it's got jelly in it."

Harry knew all of this because he had gotten so deeply into bicycle riding that he had taken a part-time job at a bike shop just to be able to talk with dedicated bike riders, some of whom were serious racers, some of whom took long, cross-country bike trips, some of whom enjoyed jumping gullies and logs and splashing through creeks on mountain trails. He had invited me to come by the shop and take a test ride on a mountain bike. I had done it and I had enjoyed it so much that I had bought my bike that day, complete with jelly seat.

I had ridden my bike regularly the previous summer over several routes I had mapped out along country roads close to my home near Asheboro, in the ancient and well worn range of central North Carolina mountains called the Uwharries. My longest run had been about 15 miles, but although the Uwharries harbored few peaks higher than 1,000 feet, they still provided some fair hills to get up my breathing and heart beat. It must have been on one of these rides that the idea of riding the parkway first presented itself.

But my bike had remained in the garage all through the fall, and I had gotten no exercise at all. As I stood leaning on my bike, breathing hard on that bright January afternoon, I realized that if I were serious about my intention of riding the parkway late in the spring, much work lay ahead of me. And not all of it was physical. It also was time to start learning about the parkway.

THE DEPRESSION'S GIFT

It had become a stock line. After every visit, just as I was reluctantly leaving, I would say, "You know, they ought to put up a statue of the person who came up with the idea for this thing."

Surely, I figured, if statues of obscure generals could be erected by the score, somewhere there should be a monument to the gentle-visioned soul who had conceived something so peace-inspiring and precious as the Blue Ridge Parkway.

If I had not been so lazy, I might have taken the time to find out who should have been depicted in that statue long before I decided to ride my bike the full distance of the parkway, but I hadn't.

When I finally began learning about the parkway and its past, I discovered that it would not be easy to decide just whose likeness that statue should bear.

Should it be that of Colonel Joseph Hyde Pratt, the head of the North Carolina Geological and Economic Survey, who in 1909 conceived a "Crest of the Blue Ridge Highway," a scenic toll road and chain of hotels stretching from Marion, Virginia, to Tallulah Falls, Georgia? Pratt actually surveyed his road and built a little section of it near Altapass in Avery County, North Carolina, before his dream was consumed by the turmoil of World War I.

Should it be that of Maurice Thatcher, a Kentucky congressman, who in the '20s wanted to build a highway connecting the national parks of Virginia, western North Carolina, Tennessee and Kentucky?

Or how about Senator Harry F. Byrd of Virginia, who, while on an inspection of a Civilian Conservation Corps camp in the Virginia mountains with President Franklin D. Roosevelt in 1933, is believed to have suggested a parkway connecting the Shenandoah and Great

Smoky Mountains national parks? Should he be the one so honored?

Then there are other claimants, all public officials of the early '30s: Thomas McDonald, chief of the Bureau of Public Roads; John Pollard, governor of Virginia; George Radcliffe, U.S. senator from Maryland; Theodore Straus, a member of the Public Works Administration.

"If I were building a monument, I would build it to the Great Depression," Harley Jolley had told me when I got around to asking him.

Jolley, a professor of history at Mars Hill College, is the authority when it comes to parkway history. A native of Lenoir, he worked for 24 years as a summer ranger and historian for the parkway, and he has written three books about it.

Whoever conceived the parkway, there is no question in Jolley's mind that the Depression built it. President Roosevelt seized the idea of the parkway as a means of putting impoverished mountain people to work and pushed it as a relief project.

As soon as funds were authorized for the project at the end of 1933, a political squabble broke out between North Carolina and Tennessee about the route the parkway would follow. Initial plans called for part of it to pass through Tennessee, but after intense lobbying by North Carolinians, a more scenic route through the southern mountains of North Carolina was chosen.

Mountain people generally welcomed the parkway, many of them willingly giving land for the right-of-way, and by 1934, surveyors were already mapping the parkway's route, much of it through rugged wilderness where no roads ever had penetrated.

On September 11, 1935, a group of dignitaries and curious mountain residents gathered at the edge of a meadow on Cumberland Knob, just south of the Virginia line. And after proper speechifying, a barbed-wire fence was snipped, and primitive bulldozers clanked across the field to begin construction of the parkway's first segment. Fifty-two years would pass before the parkway finally was finished.

Many mountain residents worked on the parkway's construction, some of them clearing land with cross saws and axes, others drilling and blasting stone or leveling roadbed with mules pulling drag pans. Hundreds of young men in Civilian Conservation Corps camps built parkway facilities with picks, spades and wheelbarrows. Highly skilled Italian and Spanish craftsmen were brought in to build retaining walls and arched bridges from native stone. Construction techniques often were unlike any ever employed in highway building, precise and cautious, often delicate, so as to preserve the natural beauty and leave no scars.

By 1940, 110 miles in Virginia and another 70 in North Carolina were open. By the mid-'50s, the parkway was largely complete, but another 59 miles in North Carolina and 34 miles in Virginia were not finished until the '60s. When a 10-mile stretch around the southern end of Asheville was opened in August of 1967, only one section remained to be built. That was a 7.2-mile segment around Grandfather Mountain. Negotiations between the National Park Service and the mountain's owner, Hugh Morton, about the route the parkway would take delayed its opening for another 20 years.

When that segment was inaugurated with a parade of old cars on a foggy day in September of 1987, the parkway finally was complete. It had cost just under $130 million to build, $25 million of that for the last seven miles, which feature a unique bridge, the Linn Cove Viaduct, that has become a tourist attraction in itself.

That a thing of such magnificent beauty and great financial benefit to the areas through which it passes should have been brought about by something so destructive and despair-filled as the Great Depression may seem high irony, but that, says Harley Jolley, is indeed the case.

"It took a special time and a special place and a special crisis to make it possible," he said.

MAKING PLANS

My plan was to start my ride along the parkway at the end of May, but after the single brief outing on my bike late in January, I wasn't sure whether I'd be able to get in good enough physical condition to keep that schedule.

Clearly, I needed to build up to some strenuous riding, but work, weather and the short daylight hours of winter conspired to keep me off my bike all through February and on into March. Instead, I climbed aboard a stationary bike several nights each week as I watched the TV news. And although I kept extending my riding times and increasing the degree of difficulty, I knew that was no substitute for tackling serious hills.

By mid-March, I was able to get out on the road some on my bike, but I rarely had time for a ride of more than 15 miles. My plan called for me to average about 30 miles a day when I started my ride along the parkway. If I could do that – and there were no problems – I could complete my ride in 16 days. But by mid-April, I still hadn't ridden my bike for 30 miles in a single stretch anywhere, not even on flat land.

On three different occasions, I loaded the bike into the back of the car and set out for the parkway, which was only two and a half hours from my house at the closest spot in Virginia. On the first trip, I broke the chain on my bike after only a few miles on the parkway and had to push the bike back to the car and bring it home for repairs.

Later, on a weekend visit with friends whose parents lived near the parkway south of Linville, North Carolina, I had managed to ride for about 10 miles before I got caught in a fierce electric storm and had to take refuge under a parkway bridge. My friends came in a station wagon to rescue me.

The third test ride was near Asheville when I went to parkway headquarters to meet officials and do research. I managed to ride for about eight miles before approaching darkness forced me to turn back to my car. So on all three test rides, I had accomplished only 30 miles of parkway riding, a single day's ride if I kept to my plan.

Early in May, my wife Linda and I headed for the parkway on a scouting mission. I didn't even bother to take the bike because I knew there would be no time for riding on this trip. We would spend a weekend driving the entire length of the parkway, something that neither of us ever had done. Our purpose was to determine just how feasible this adventure of mine would be. We would be judging terrain, scouting campgrounds, searching out watering holes and the like.

To this point, my intention had been to rough it on my ride. I would sleep under the stars in parkway campgrounds, prepare my meals by the side of the road. I already had accumulated all the necessary gear: saddle bags for my bike, a compact tent, sleeping bag, bedroll, sterno stove, mess gear, dual water bottles to fit on the frame of my bike, a book on bike repairs, a repair kit, an air pump, two small and expensive flashlights. Linda had not been especially keen on this idea of roughing it, afraid that something might happen to me, but I assured her that I would be fine.

The parkway was beautiful as we began our scouting mission at its beginning in Virginia. Many of the trees were still pastel green. Dogwoods and redbuds were in bloom. We came upon wild pink azaleas and fields of wild flowers just breaking into bloom.

But only 14 miles along the parkway, a loud knocking erupted in the car's engine and I cut the ignition and pulled onto the grass. We had taken the car in for a tune-up and full service just before leaving so that any potential problems could be spotted and corrected, and here we were, broken down on the parkway, miles from any town, and nothing in sight but woods.

What little traffic there was passed without slowing, as I poked around helplessly under the hood. Across a big grassy field, I saw an occasional hiker emerge from the woods, burdened by a backpack, and trudge on northward, following the Appalachian Trail, no help at all to me. I was about to set out hiking myself in search of a side road, a house, a telephone, when a green Park Service truck stopped on the opposite side of the road, and a friendly, freckled, sandy-haired ranger got out and asked if he could be of help.

"Boy, am I glad to see you," I said, telling him what had happened. He looked under the hood and quickly spotted the problem.

"You've thrown a spark plug," he said.

The engine had spit out one of the new spark plugs, installed only the day before. The ranger tried to put it back into its socket but succeeded only in burning his hand on the hot engine parts. We finally got it back into the aperture, but neither of us could tighten it with the few tools we had on hand.

"We need a plug wrench," the ranger said, and went to his truck to radio headquarters to see if one could be located. While we waited, I mentioned the bike ride I was my planning, and he told me about the longest and most arduous climbs that I would face. If I made it over Apple Orchard Mountain, the first of these climbs, I'd probably make it the whole distance, he said. Apple Orchard Mountain was about 60 miles south. Many bicyclists who set out to conquer the entire parkway from the northern end quit on Apple Orchard Mountain, he noted.

As we talked, several motorcycles passed, and the ranger remarked that the parkway had become the most popular road in the country with motorcyclists. More and more were coming to the parkway all the time, he said, and some were not returning. He had seen several fatal motorcycle accidents. In one recent year, seven of the 10 traffic fatalities on the parkway had been motorcyclists.

"What about bicyclists?" I asked, not bothering to conceal my anxiety.

He was seeing more bicyclists, too, he said, sometimes in large groups, and although he remembered a few minor accidents and close calls by bicyclists, he couldn't recall one being killed on the parkway.

"That's a relief," I said.

Nobody at headquarters could find a spark plug wrench, and the ranger suggested that I leave the parkway and try to find one in the nearest little community, Sherando. We could coast down the mountain to the highway, he said, and if we took it easy we probably could make it to a gas station and have the spark plug reinstalled.

We made it down the mountain without problem and turned toward Sherando with the engine clicking merrily along. There was no sign of a gas station or any other business. But after a few miles we passed a house where four men were working on a battered race car in front of a backyard garage. I pulled in behind the race car and all four men turned at the sound coming from my engine.

"Sounds bad," one said, after I had cut off the ignition and got out of the car. I explained the problem, and without speaking another word, the man walked into the garage, where I could hear him rattling through tool boxes. Shortly, he returned carrying a spark plug wrench. All four men gathered somberly to watch while he tightened the loose plug and checked all the others.

"That ought to do it," he said. "See how it sounds."

I cranked the car and the engine purred smoothly.

"How much do I owe you?" I said.

"Nothin'," he replied. "Y'all just have a good trip."

Soon we were back up the mountain and headed south again on the parkway, feeling good about nature and neighborly strangers. We made many stops and took lots of side roads to see what was down them. I began filling a legal pad with notes, taking particular notice of facilities available near the junctions of my planned 30-mile travel segments. Often there was nothing but wilderness.

By late afternoon, we had driven fewer than 150 miles along the parkway and still had 130 to go if we were to reach Deep Gap in North Carolina and find a room and dinner in Boone, as we had planned. Clearly, we would have to cut out side-road trips, make fewer stops and pick up the pace. Even then it would be well after dark by the time we got there.

Then, 30 miles south of Roanoke, climbing into a sharp curve, we came upon flares blazing in the roadway.

"Something has happened," Linda said, as I slowed the car.

As we got deeper into the curve, I could see a fire truck and two rescue squad vehicles with emergency lights flashing. The road was littered with debris. People were scurrying about.

The scene took a moment to register as I stopped the car. Then I realized that the big hunk of wreckage on the edge of the northbound lane had been a motorcycle. And just behind it lay a body covered with a rumpled blue sheet.

"Oh, no, Jerry," Linda said. "I don't want to see this."

"Somebody must have hit it head-on," I said, but no other vehicle was in sight.

For a minute we sat with the engine running, uncertain what to do. Clearly we could be of no help. My inclination was to drive on by and try to put the awful scene out of mind as quickly as possible, but I couldn't see around the curve to tell if we could get by the wreckage.

"I'm going to have to walk up there and check," I said.

I was only a short distance from the car when I saw that the wreck was worse than I had thought. A second body, covered by a yellow tarp, lay on the edge of the southbound lane about 30 feet from the remains of the motorcycle. A motorcyclist's black helmet was in the ditch, 15 feet beyond the body. Somebody had placed a tan woman's pocketbook beside the body, and atop the tarp lay a driver's license with a middle-aged woman's face smiling from it.

Both bodies lay ignored as rescue workers rushed about, tending to others. Several hovered over a prone young man wrapped in a gray blanket. A woman was inserting an IV into his arm. Another young man, shirtless, wearing camouflage pants and boots, his head and body streaked with blood, sat on the roadside a few feet from the sheet-covered body at the back of the motorcycle. Yet another young man had an arm around his shoulder, comforting him.

Twenty-five feet down an embankment, an upended new Ford pickup truck, black and meticulously clean, was wrapped around a tree. Most of the rescue workers were clustered around the crushed cab of the truck, where a young woman was trapped.

"She's still alive," a rescue worker said to me without my asking a word as he rushed past to fetch a needed piece of equipment.

The motorcycle had been a big and fancy one, pulling a small trailer which had split open, spewing its contents over the roadway. A small fiberglass storage compartment, splintered now, perched on the back of the motorcycle above the Baldwin County, Ga., license tag, and on it was a neatly painted sign, the kind people put on campers to express their openness and pride: "The Crawfords," it said. "Martha and Jimmy."

Suddenly, the covered bodies had identities, and walking among their scattered personal belongings, I felt as if I were violating their privacy and started back to my car.

Later, I would learn that Martha and Jimmy Crawford had been high school sweethearts in Wrightsville, Ga. They married right out of high school and two years later a son, Randy, was born. A daughter, Terri, followed after another two years. Jimmy went into electrical work and eventually started his own business as an electrician. Martha worked with him, keeping the books, sending bills, and later their son also joined the business. The Crawfords worked hard and prospered. By their middle years, they had a pretty brick house in the country, five miles outside Milledgeville; four grandchildren – Randy's boy and Terri's three girls, the pride of their lives – and a big Honda Gold Wing motorcycle that both loved.

Jimmy Crawford's interest in motorcycles was of long standing. He would buy one, keep it for a while, sell it. He sometimes went for long periods without one, but he always returned to them. Five years earlier, he had bought his first Gold Wing – a fancy, comfortable, smooth-riding touring motorcycle – and he and Martha started riding with a local club of Gold Wing owners. They loved it and often toured with the group to other states.

"They were safe, very, very safe riders," their daughter later would tell me. "They were the type who never rode close to dark, never rode in rain, never rode in wind...."

Two years earlier, Jimmy had bought a new Gold Wing with fancier gadgets on it, and he had his and Martha's names painted across the back. They liked traveling on it so much that they often took spur-of-the-moment trips, just the two of them.

The day before, Martha had called her daughter in Americus, Ga., two hours from Milledgeville, to tell her that she and Jimmy had decided to take off to the Blue Ridge Parkway. They would be back in four days. She had sounded happy and excited about the trip.

"Y'all be careful," Terri had told her. "We love you."

They were the last words she would speak to her mother.

Motorcyclists in large numbers, including many Gold Wing riders, were rallying in Cherokee at the southern end of the parkway that weekend, but late that Saturday afternoon, the Crawfords had crossed into Virginia and were riding leisurely northward along the parkway, nearly 300 miles from the big gathering.

At about 4:30, they had stopped at the Rocky Knob Visitors Center at Milepost 169. They were dressed identically in blue jeans, cowboy boots and light tan jackets. The afternoon had begun to turn cool, and they wanted to find a room before the chill made riding unpleasant.

Laura Bandkau, a ranger who was beginning her second season on the parkway, told them that they had just passed a couple of places five miles back. The next motels were in Roanoke, 50 miles northward.

Laura and the Crawfords chatted for a few minutes, talking about where the Crawfords were from, their grandchildren, the parkway, the weather, the distance to Roanoke. They thanked Laura and left with smiles.

Warm, friendly people, Laura thought. Made her think of her grandparents. If only everybody who stopped at the visitor center could be so nice.

At 5:10, Laura closed the center and went to her government quarters nearby. She was standing outside when another ranger, Randal Griffin, called to tell her that there had been an accident near Milepost 151.

The rangers arrived at the scene with blue lights flashing, and as soon as Laura saw the motorcycle in the road she recognized it.

"I was just talking with these people," she said, the shock showing in her voice.

The carnage before them was nothing new to Randal Griffin. This was the third double-fatality motorcycle wreck he'd seen in the past three years on the 70-mile stretch of the parkway that he patrolled.

The rescue workers had freed the young woman, whose name, I later learned, was Ravena Holliday. She was 20 and from Salem, Virginia, near Roanoke. The workers were placing her carefully on a spine board. The two injured young men, James Hart, also 20, also from Salem, and Mark Drinkard, who was 19 and from Mechanicsville, Virginia, were being loaded into ambulances. All were students at nearby Ferrum College. They had been on an outing at a waterfall near the parkway. A blood-drenched jam box sat upright on the roadside near Jimmy Crawford's black cowboy boots, which were standing neatly aligned beside his body.

"Is this your car?" Randal Griffin asked me.

"Yes."

"Would you mind moving it? I need these skid marks."

The skid marks indicated that the truck had gone into the motorcycle's lane.

I'd seen more than I wanted and asked if the wreck could be bypassed. Randal Griffin directed me to a detour. I told Linda what I had seen as we made our way over narrow, twisting dirt roads down the mountain from the wreck, emerging again onto the parkway about a mile beyond the sobering sights behind us. Once again the parkway was tranquil and beautiful, goldenly radiant in the waning daylight. Sudden death and destruction seemed incongruous, if not impossible, in such a setting.

Yet, as we rode along in silence, absorbing the magnificent views, I couldn't help but think that these were the last views the Crawfords had seen, and I knew what was on Linda's mind, for it was on my mind, too: that could be me lying dead in a ditch, my tangled bike at the parkway's edge.

But that fear was not spoken until the next day, after we had finished our mission along the parkway and were heading back home from Cherokee. As we had continued westward on the parkway, we had heard the story of another bicyclist, about 50, who had died of a heart attack while attempting to peddle along the parkway up the side of Mount Mitchell, the highest mountain in the East.

Clearly, there was risk in this trip I had planned. And the scouting mission had shown that there were other difficulties as well. Campgrounds and other facilities often were much farther apart than I had anticipated and inconveniently situated to match my planned schedule of 30 miles per day. If I did rough it, I would have to slip off into the woods to camp, which not only was against the rules but provided no comforts. I might be without shelter in storms and bad weather.

We discussed all of this on the way home, particularly the concerns for safety, and by the time we got back, the plan for my trip had been rather drastically altered.

I wouldn't rough it after all. I'd spend my nights in motels or lodges. And I wouldn't be traveling alone. Linda would go with me in the car. She would let me out at my starting spot each morning, meet me along the way for lunch. We even could ride off the parkway to restaurants in nearby towns if we wanted.

If my ride for the day happened to end far from any lodging place, she would pick me up and carry me to wherever we planned to stay.

Linda's presence not only would make the trip more comfortable, it would make it safer as well. On the most arduous climbs, she would wait at overlooks along the way to offer cold drinks and encouragement – and to make certain that I made it without keeling over.

True, my trip would not be quite as adventurous this way, but it would be far easier, less lonely and much more fun. And the challenge of riding 470 miles of mountains still was formidable, so formidable, after seeing what lay ahead of me, that I had serious doubts that I could make it.

STARTING OUT: Author Jerry Bledsoe is ready for his adventure along the Blue Ridge Parkway, beginning at Rockfish Gap, Virginia.

DAY ONE

If not for the sign, you wouldn't know that you were leaving one road and embarking upon another. Skyline Drive sweeps grandly down from the Shenandoah National Park to Rockfish Gap, a place of spectacular beauty, and assumes a new identity.

Here, where vistas open on both sides of Afton Mountain – west the Shenandoah Valley, east the Rockfish River Valley – here, where Thomas Jefferson came in 1818 to decide the location of the University of Virginia, the Blue Ridge Parkway begins.

And here, well after noon on a Sunday, Memorial Day Weekend, of all times, the beginning of the summer vacation season, one of the busiest weekends every year along the parkway, I came to start my ride.

I had intended to be here a day earlier, and at a much earlier hour, but last-minute frustrations had caused us to get a late start from home, and we had arrived the day before too late to start the ride. That had caused another problem. All rooms near the parkway were taken. Neither had we been able to find one in nearby Waynesboro, or in Staunton, or at more than a dozen places we had tried in and around Charlottesville. Finally, nearing midnight, as I was despairing that we might have to spent the night in the car, a harried desk clerk in a Charlottesville hotel, seeing my desperation, offered me a room that had been hurriedly abandoned by its previous occupants for reasons unknown. There were cracker crumbs on the mussed bed, cigarette butts in the ash trays, dirty glasses on the nightstands and some of the towels had been used, but we had been grateful for a place to lay our heads.

Before embarking on my ride, I stopped in at the Rockfish Gap

Tourist Information Bureau near the parkway entrance and asked one of the women working there how Rockfish Gap got its name.

"I can give you half a dozen versions," Lillian Canody told me, "but I don't know which one you want."

Lillian, I learned with a little more questioning, was born just down the mountain before the Blue Ridge Parkway was conceived. A Goodloe, she was then, from a family with long lineage in the area. As a young woman, she married, moved away and was gone for more than 30 years. Retirement had brought her back home 14 years earlier.

"You come back here and everything's different," she said. "Used to be, if somebody asked directions, you never told them how far it was, you just went by the farms. Start at Afton, my Uncle Jim had a hostel there then. Then you come to the Lipscombs, then the Myerses, then the Wade place. All those places are gone now. I guess that's progress. But this is still my favorite place in the whole world."

That was one reason she had gone to work as a volunteer at the information center. She enjoyed telling people about this area, hoping they would come to appreciate it as much as she does. But she couldn't say for sure how the gap got its name.

"Some say it was because of a kind of fish they caught in the river here," she said. "Some say there was a man named Roche who lived near here and named it."

She turned to her friend and fellow volunteer, Jean Hubbard, a transplanted West Virginian whose great-grandfather sat on the jury that tried John Brown.

"What's your version?"

"Had something to do with the Indians, didn't it?" said Jean.

"Wish we could tell you more," Lillian said with a shrug as I thanked her for her help.

It was 12:45 when I rolled my bike up to the sign that told of some of the historical highlights of Rockfish Gap and posed with my bike while Linda snapped my picture.

I strapped on my foam-lined plastic helmet and straddled my bike.

"Well, here I go," I said.

"Just be careful," Linda replied.

The elevation at Rockfish Gap is 1,909 feet and the parkway begins with an uphill ride. I started in a middle gear and the climb was gradual enough that I pedaled seated. Linda watched me leave, then got into the car and passed me with a wave and a toot of the horn. We'd arranged to meet for lunch at a picnic area eight and a half miles away.

It was a fine day, clear and hazy, the temperature in the mid 80s. There was a gentle, cooling breeze and I hadn't even started to work up a sweat when I reached the first overlook, just two tenths of a mile from the parkway's beginning, but 145 feet higher. Far below, I could see the tiny community of Afton, and it caused me to sing a few lines from an old song imbedded in my childhood, "Flow Gently, Sweet Afton," as I headed onward and upward. By the time, I had reached Mile Post 1, the grade had increased, and I was out of the saddle pedaling.

"Four hundred and sixty nine to go," I said to the marker as I passed.

Another overlook, this one offering a view of the Rockfish River Valley, presented itself a half mile later, at 2,150 feet, and I paused to drink in the scenery and take a sip of the cold Gatorade that I had put into one of my water bottles.

The climb continued for another mile and a half, and the traffic was heavy, cars zipping past one after another, causing me to keep a close eye on the rear-view mirror I had installed on my left handlebar. Most of the cars gave me wide berth, however.

At Mile Post 3, I got a cooling downhill run, past blooming rhododendron, for a full mile to a short leveling, then another brisk downhill ride to Mile Post 5, where a steep, sweat-producing climb began. Dewberries were in bloom along the roadside, but I was having to work too hard to appreciate them.

The Humpback Rocks Visitor Center offered a break in the climb a half mile farther on. Here a pioneer homestead has been reconstructed. The parking lot was crowded with cars. People wandered through the exhibits. Smoke rose from the stone chimney of the log cabin. I noticed on a sign that fire building was one of the day's demonstrations. Storytelling and a talk about mountain social life also were on the agenda, but none of the events was scheduled conveniently for my itinerary.

I took my camera from a saddlebag to snap a few pictures, and when I returned to my bike, I found two skinny-tired-bicycle riders in brightly colored tight shorts examining it. They turned out to be from England, Durham City, friendly fellows. They were "on holiday," and they had rented bikes in Reston, near Washington, ridden down Skyline Drive and made it this far on the parkway, but they soon were going to have to turn back to catch a flight home. Neither had ever seen

GREENSTONE OVERLOOK: One skinny little tree seems to be the only thing preventing this boulder from falling.

CATCHING THE WIND: A hang glider waits to take off from Ravens Roost. A few minutes later, he fell from his perch, but wasn't injured.

a mountain bike and they quizzed me about it. I offered to let them ride it, and they took turns wheeling gleefully around the parking area. I got the distinct impression that both were tired of riding hunched over, but I was too polite to inquire how they felt about their riding pants and whether they, too, were rented.

In the next three uphill miles, I passed three dead snakes – two copperheads and a huge black snake – caught a stunning view of the Shenandoah Valley off to the west, and just 45 minutes after leaving Linda at the beginning of the parkway, I arrived at the Humpback Rocks Recreation Area, where we were to meet for lunch.

Linda had chosen an open picnic table near several that had been taken over for a big family gathering. There must have been 25 or 30 people in the group, the elders resting in lawn chairs, the children running and yelling at play. Two tables had been spread with great mounds of food: potato salad, green beans, corn on the cob, deviled eggs, cakes, pies, big jugs of iced tea and lemonade. Two striped watermelons chilled in a tub of ice.

The patriarch of the clan, a robust man with white hair, a boisterous voice and a wide smile, presided over a big grill barbecuing chicken. He kept teasing the children as they swirled playfully around him.

The aromas were excruciating as I laid out our fare: two cans of Beanee-Weenees, two plastic spoons and crackers with processed cheese spread.

"I'm going to go ask if I can eat with them," Linda said.

Just after 3:00, Linda and I parted again, she driving on to the little inn we had discovered on one of our side trips off the parkway a few weeks earlier.

"If I'm not there by dark, come looking for me," I said.

"You'd better be there a long time before dark," she said.

Just a third of a mile from the picnic area, I stopped at Greenstone Overlook, named for a type of stone with a deep, greenish hue, formed from an ancient lava flow, that underlies the first miles of the parkway. A marked trail looping from the parking area tells the story of the geology, but I didn't have time to take it all in. I did pause long enough to take a photo of a huge, fascinating boulder in the parking area. It was balanced at such an acute angle that it seemed about to topple at any moment. Only a skinny little tree that had valiantly flattened itself against the rock seemed to be holding it back.

I had only a brief downhill run before starting another 1.7-mile climb to Ravens Roost, elevation 3,200 feet, my highest point so far. As I neared the overlook, I saw so many cars pulled to the side of the road that I thought I might be coming upon another accident. It was instead an accident waiting to happen.

A big crowd had gathered around the rugged rock outcropping at the overlook. People were lined along a stone wall, looking toward the Shenandoah Valley far below. At first, I couldn't see what they were looking at. I did see the ravens that normally roost on this mountain soaring high above the valley, but I soon discovered that they were not the reason so many people had gathered.

Perched on the edge of the cliff beyond the rock wall was another would-be soarer, a young man burdened with a parachute and supporting a big yellow kite. Ravens Roost, I learned, is one of only two sites on the parkway where hang gliders are allowed to leap into space (the other is at Roanoke Mountain) and soar like the ravens before landing in one of the few available spots, tiny patches of pale green field in a sea of deep green forest, far below and miles away.

I parked my bike, got out my camera and joined a group of spectators on the rock outcropping. By questioning bystanders, I learned that the young man waiting to take off was named Morgan, and he was from the Virgin Islands, visiting friends in Charlottesville. He was hesitant, dissatisfied with the winds, cautious and uncertain. He kept moving to the cliff's edge, then stepping back and squatting to wait. A young woman, one of his friends from Charlottesville, and a new acquaintance, a young man from Australia, stood alongside the glider keeping its wings from tipping.

Five minutes passed, then 10. The young man remained hesitant. The crowd grew restless. Remembering Linda's admonishment, I decided that I didn't have time to wait any longer and returned to my bike. Just as I was putting my camera away, I heard a loud, collective gasp.

Somebody screamed. People started running toward the rock.

"He crashed," said a young man running past me, seeking the path to the cliff.

I followed him back onto the rocks. As I went past the rock wall, a woman was pulling at her children, saying, "Come on, let's go. I don't want to see this." On the cliff, people were on hands and knees, peering anxiously over the edge.

"What happened?" I asked a man standing near the edge.

"Looked like he lost his footing in that gravel and just went right over the edge," he said. "He didn't take off, he just fell."

From as close to the edge as I dared, I could see no sign of the young man in the trees 100 feet or so below.

The young man's friends were yelling over the edge of the cliff, talking, I discovered, to some climbers on the rocks below who had seen the fall.

"He's talking," one of his companions called to others with relief.

"He's okay," somebody yelled from below. His fall apparently had been broken enough by the glider to keep him from being seriously hurt.

"Okay," a young man called snidely to the staring crowd, "show's over, everybody can leave now."

As I was leaving a little later, the young woman from Charlottesville was yelling over the cliff about the glider, which was no longer in condition to allow anybody to soar like a raven. "You want us to get a rope to bring it back up?"

It was a swift three-mile run downhill from the roost to Reed's Gap, where I again encountered the two English fellows I had met earlier, taking a break. They called out and waved as I passed, and one of them snapped a photo of me. The next four miles were up and down, never varying more than 100 feet in altitude. I began to notice that my legs were tiring, and I had a twinge of pain in my right side, brought on, no doubt, from not taking in enough oxygen on my uphill runs. I paused to rest at the Priest overlook.

The Priest, a 4,059-foot peak, rose to the south, between Main Top Mountain to the west and Three Ridges Mountain to the east. Beyond the Priest, out of sight, I knew from my parkway map, lay a string of other religiously named mountains, the Friar, the Cardinal, the Bald Friar. Nobody's sure how these mountains came to bear these names, but it's thought that the Priest was named for a man named Priest, and jokesters named the others to give the Priest company.

After a one-mile, 150-foot descent, I climbed 166 feet over the next half mile to Twenty Minute Cliff, so called, according to the sign at the overlook, because people in the community of White Rock in the valley below use the stone face of the mountain as a time piece during June and July. Twenty minutes after sunlight strikes the cliffs on the mountain's western side, dusk falls in the valley below. White Rock appeared to be sparsely populated, for only one tiny house was visible.

While I was enjoying this view, a car stopped, and two young men and a young woman got out and struck up a conversation.

"You've got to be from England," I said after hearing their accents.

"How on earth did you know?" asked one of the young men, laughing, then admitting that they were from London.

"It's just that everybody I've met on the parkway today has been from England," I said, going on to tell them about the two bicyclists I'd passed again just a few miles back.

Climbing again, I passed an area where wild pink azaleas were blooming on both sides of the road. As I struggled on, sweating and straining for breath, a whole team of young bicyclists, wearing identical uniforms and helmets, appeared around a curve ahead, hunched over their low-slung handlebars and bunched tightly, racing downhill so fast that they passed in a blur. I didn't even have time to count them, 12, maybe 15. Their tires made a roaring sound as they passed.

This climb continued for four miles and 600 feet in altitude, and I had to pull onto the shoulder a couple of times to catch my breath and take a slug of tepid water (I'd already finished off my Gatorade). On one of those stops, looking back, I could follow the path of the parkway for miles along the ridges. It looked as if it would be an awfully tough ride on a bicycle, but actually it hadn't seemed so bad. I finally topped out at the highest elevation I had achieved so far, 3,294 feet, at an overlook offering a view of Fork Mountain, which was 50 feet lower than the spot where I stood.

A brief descent took me to another climb into high, open meadows and a calendar view of a two-story, tin-roofed farm house with a hemlock tree in front, a weeping willow in back, an apple tree by the pig lot and a big barn up on the ridge. Another descent took me to my final climb of the day, to a bald ridge that early settlers called the War Fields because of all the arrowheads they found there.

I dawdled at the overlook, enjoying the grand view and the early evening breeze, regretting that my ride was about to come to the end for the day. It had been a grand day, actually, if I overlooked lunch, but I knew that dinner would be better, and it awaited me only a few miles away, and a few hundred feet down the mountainside.

The ride from the War Fields to Virginia Highway 56 at Tye River Gap was less than a mile, but a 215-foot drop in elevation. The descent, however, was nothing to compare to the one on Highway 56. I had to brake all the way to keep from building up so much speed that I couldn't make the curves. In a matter of minutes, I had reached the sharp, steep turnoff to the rustic lodge where Linda was waiting.

I had to continue braking on this narrow lane, which was even steeper and more treacherous than the highway I'd just left. But then I crossed the wooden bridge over Little Mary's Creek, a wonderfully vigorous and noisy stream, and ahead of me was an incline so steep that when I attempted it, the front wheel of my bike rose from the pavement like a bucking bronco and almost threw me. I did the prudent thing, dismounted and pushed my bike up to the stone wall in front of the two-story log building, where Linda stood laughing on the porch.

"That last hill too much for you?" she asked.

"I don't see how a car gets up it," I said.

A short time later, we were sitting in rocking chairs on the porch enjoying a drink and watching the sun set behind the tall trees. After a wonderful dinner of shrimp with black olives, feta cheese and fresh tomatoes, I sat before the huge stone fireplace in the lodge's great room, chatting with the inn's owners, Smokey and Gena Schroeder.

They told me that the twisting lane to the lodge was covered with ice when they first came down it a few days before Christmas in 1983, and they weren't sure that they wanted to entrust their lives to it. But they did it at the insistence of their son, Larry, who wanted them to see this place he had told them about. When they had made it safely up that final, sharp rise, they liked what they saw.

"It was different,' said Smokey.

"It's one of a kind, there's no doubt about it," Gena said.

"It had lots of possibilities," Smokey added.

What stood before them was a small community of buildings that Richard Meeth had set high into the western face of South Mountain. Richard was a theologian who as a seminarian helped his grandfather restore an old log cabin on Rockbridge Mountain. That led him to later restore an old mill in the Shenandoah Valley and to begin to collect decaying old log buildings around the countryside.

He acquired three cabins in Buffalo Creek, a two-story house in Fairfield, a barn in Vesuvius, a small school in Churchville and the general store in Raphine where Cyrus McCormick, the inventor of the reaper, once traded. All of these he disassembled, carefully numbering and storing the logs. His intention was to bring them all back together in a house for himself on 27 acres he had bought on South Mountain.

He hired a crew of 18 skilled mountain men to build the house and

THE SUGAR TREE INN: Smokey and Gena Schroeder (right), daughter Karla and her husband Keith Painter, and their daughter Emily.

a crew of mountain women to chink the logs. When they had finished, he realized that he had built more than he needed. This was big enough to be a lodge, and he decided to turn it into an inn.

He got his workmen to build a big porch across the front of the structure, add a kitchen onto the back, a solarium for a dining room. Then he got them to build a four-room guest house just down the hill with the leftover logs, and just beyond that, another more conventional guest house, and down by the creek a gate cottage.

When he had finished, he had three guest rooms in the lodge, four in each guest house and two in the gate cottage, each with a stone fireplace, and all spacious and appropriately furnished with antiques.

He named his creation Sugar Tree Inn and opened it in 1981. Two years later, he was dead from a car crash on a nearby road. The inn was closed and for sale when Gena and Smokey Schroeder first drove down that twisting lane to see it.

Gena, a watercolorist who has sold her paintings widely, and Smokey, a retired Air Force officer who then was working for a medical electronics company, lived near Mount Vernon, outside Alexandria, Virginia, and traveled frequently, usually staying in country inns.

Never had they seen an inn like this one, though, and by spring they were its proud new owners. Their son managed it for them in the first months until his sister, Karla, who as a teenager danced with the American Ballet Theater, could come and assume those duties.

Smokey kept his job, and he and Gena commuted to the inn to help out on weekends. Business was good. They often rented all 13 rooms and had dozens of additional people for dinner. Smokey and Gena found themselves staying longer and doing more and more.

"It became so much work that we decided that wasn't what we wanted," Gena said. "We've changed each year to get it to the quiet mountain inn that we have now."

Among the changes: dropping their liquor license, denying credit cards, declining to accept so many dinner reservations, cutting back the number of guest rooms and letting all employees go.

The year before, Smokey and Gena sold their house near Alexandria and moved to the inn to make it strictly a family operation. Gena took on the duties of attending the guests with the help of their daughter, Dawn, who lives next to the lodge with her two children. Smokey started tending the grounds, cutting the firewood, fixing what needed fixing. Karla became the chef, helped by her husband, Keith Painter.

Smokey and Gena keep the inn open only from late April until early November, and only seven rooms are ever rented, three in the lodge and four in the log guest house. There are no TVs, radios, newspapers. After dinner, if the evening is cool, guests often gather to chat around the big fireplace, as we were doing. If the evening is warm, they usually find rocking chairs on the front porch, as we had earlier.

"You really slow down up here," said Gena. "It takes about one night."

"We can look out our window when it's getting dark and see the deer coming down the mountain," said Smokey.

The tranquility that leads guests to slow down had not been without effect on the inn's owners, I discovered.

"I sometimes sit here and think about turning this into a house," Gena told me. "You know, this would make a beautiful house."

Trip Progress Log, Day One: 27 miles
27 total miles completed, 442 to go.

DAY TWO

The second day of my trip began much as the first had, pedaling uphill, but this time the slope was gentler and I got an earlier start. The day, like the one before, was clear and hot, with the distant mountains fading into a gauzy haze.

After less than a mile of easy climbing, I reached level roadway and wheeled into the Whetstone Ridge Recreation Area at Mile Post 29. Once, mountaineers made their way here to dig from the mountain the fine-grained stones that they used to sharpen their knives and tools. Now only tourists stop at the Park Service concession to buy gas, sandwiches and souvenirs.

I struck up a conversation with Doris Bryant, who told me that she had worked at the coffee shop here for 19 years, rising from waitress to manager. The parkway looms large in her life, Doris said. Her husband, Milton, had worked for 22 years as a maintenance man on the parkway. Yet the only part of the parkway that Doris ever sees, she said, are the two miles of it that she drives to work from her home in Montebello, five miles away.

"We have got on it and went from here to Vinton," she said, a distance of about 75 miles, "but that's as far as we've been. My husband says he works on it and he don't need to ride on it. I would like to go the whole way sometime, though. I hope to someday."

Two and a half miles from Whetstone Ridge, I passed through Still House Hollow, once the site of a legal distillery where farmers brought their grain to be turned into tax-paid spirits. No still brings distinction to this place now, but the hemlocks do. They tower over the roadway, and their trunks are so huge that I couldn't reach halfway around one.

Climbing toward Mile Post 32, I pedaled under a canopy of tree limbs overgrowing the parkway, giving it the darkness and coolness of a tunnel. Still climbing at Mile Post 33, I kept dodging caterpillars. The parkway was literally crawling with caterpillars of several varieties, thousands and thousands of them, and the road surface was splattered with their squished carcasses. This was a phenomenon I had noticed from the beginning of my trip. Why they were drawn to the pavement, I had no idea, but clearly, with all this caterpillar carnage, the parkway was depriving the world of millions, maybe billions of butterflies and moths.

At the Yankee Horse Ridge parking area, I stopped to examine a stretch of narrow gauge railroad track that had been put here as an exhibit, a monument to human exploitation of these mountains. This section of track had once been part of a 50-mile line over which more than 100 million board feet of logs had been hauled early in this century. Almost no virgin forest was left anywhere in the Appalachians. But plenty of trees grew here now, second growth, forever protected from loggers, and a lively little creek named Wigwam flowed beneath them and under the track. I followed the stream uphill along a short trail to a noisy waterfall so beautiful that I just wanted to sit and watch it, lost in its music.

But I reluctantly returned to my bike and pushed on, descending rapidly over the next three miles to Irish Gap, then climbing again to the Boston Knob Overlook, where I stopped once again to study an exhibit about birds.

More than 100 varieties of birds can be seen along the parkway, many of them migratory species that appear mainly in spring and late summer, I read. The scarlet tanager, I learned, flies back and forth each year from countries on the west coast of South America, the red-eyed vireo from Brazil, the indigo bunting from Cuba. I'd never seen any of these birds, as far as I knew, but I was familiar with most of those that were permanent residents along the parkway: mocking bird, goldfinch, chickadee, nut hatch, cardinal, towhee, titmouse, woodpecker, raven, vulture, red-tailed hawk.

Just three miles farther on, after I had pulled over to a shady spot to take off my helmet and cool my overheating head, I saw a flash of iridescent blue in a nearby tree and moved closer for a better look. There on a limb sat an indigo bunting, the first I'd ever seen. I recognized it immediately from the illustration at the exhibit, and I was glad I had taken the time to stop and study it. If that dainty bird could fly here all the way from Cuba, I told myself, I surely could make it to the end of the parkway on a bicycle.

Ten minutes later, I was on the side of the road again after suffering the first mishap of the trip. A big, black beetle had flown directly into my path as I was making a short descent at a good clip. It had hit me squarely in the right eye. My eye was hurting so bad I could barely open it, and when I did, everything from that eye was a blur. I washed the eye from my water bottle, and the pain gradually eased as my vision cleared. I could see in my rear-view mirror, though, that the eye was red and I was afraid that it was bruised. Who would believe that a beetle gave me a black eye?

Linda rescued me for lunch a short time later, and we drove ahead to the coffee shop at the Otter Creek concession area for cheeseburgers. Afterward, she returned me to my stopping place and I gave her an estimated arrival time to meet me at the James River, my destination for this day. It would be a relatively easy ride, for I would be descending nearly 2,000 feet over the next 18 miles. But I had learned one truth about the parkway. It almost never descended completely. It descended some, went back up a little, descended some more, and so on. Even when it was carrying you down, it almost always demanded some climbing.

One of those climbs came after I had crossed U.S. 60. It led up to an overlook with a view of Buena Vista, an old iron mining town, where we had ventured for gas and food on our scouting mission along the parkway.

Another climb began at Indian Gap, this one of 400 feet spread over two miles, and the sweat that seeped out of my headband was burning my sore eye by the time I reached the view of the House Mountains, where Carolina rhododendron grew from the bare rock outcroppings.

From the time I had come onto the parkway, I had been aware that the Appalachian Trail never had been very far away. It more or less parallels the parkway for its first 100 miles and crosses it numerous times, the passages marked by slashes of white paint on roadside trees. I had noticed a couple of those crossings near the beginning of the parkway, and just past Mile Post 51, I again saw the familiar trail markings on trees on the right side of the road. A short distance farther down the hill, the markings appeared again on the left.

There, ensconced like some wilderness king, a big man sat in a folding lawn chair. He wore heavy hiking boots and shorts held up by blue suspenders. Around his head was a red, white and blue sweatband and around his knees elastic braces ("Downhill knee," he would later explain). A pipe was clenched between his teeth; another lay beside his chair. A package of tobacco bulged from the pocket of his t-shirt. A trail map lay nearby, but he was reading a paperback book, *Wilderness Empire* by Allan W. Eckert.

Intrigued, I stopped and introduced myself. His name, I learned, was John Goodhart. Earlier in the day, he had hiked up to Punchbowl Shelter, a fairly steep climb, and now he was just resting and waiting to see if any other hikers passed his way.

"I haven't been hiking as much as I used to," he said. "Just sort of lazy. I used to hike every weekend."

He was 51, he said, and had been hiking for 10 years, almost all of it on the Appalachian Trail. He took his first hike against his will when he and his wife, Diana, were on a trip to the Shenandoah Valley.

"She browbeat me into hiking, and I liked it so much that we took a backpacking class at the community college."

Soon he was hiking frequently, and he joined the Roanoke Appalachian Trail Club, one of more than 30 clubs that maintain the 2,100-mile trail in the 14 states through which it passes on its way from Springer Mountain, Ga., to Mount Katahdin, Maine. Nearly a fourth of the trail is in Virginia, John explained, and he was personally responsible for upkeep along a 10-mile stretch in Giles County near the West Virginia border.

John said that he and his fellow club members work on the trail 16 weekends each year. They cut back growth, clear obstacles, repair damage, install barriers to erosion, build bridges and fences, divert little streams. Sometimes they even reroute the trail.

"It's a constant thing," he said. "Last year, our club put in five-thousand, five-hundred man hours on the trail. I just felt I had an obligation that if I were going to use the trail, I should put something back into it. You know, last year they estimated that over one million people hiked on some portion of the Appalachian Trail. That's an awful lot of people."

Just then a car pulled up, and a hiker got out with a heavy pack, thanking the driver for the ride. Fred Pittman of Hendersonville, North Carolina, had left his car at this crossing. Its license tag read "BAC-PACKER."

TRAIL MAN: Appalachian Trail hiker John Goodhart takes a break at a spot where the Appalachian Trail crosses the Blue Ridge Parkway.

"How far'd you go?" John called to him.

"I started here Friday evening about three and went thirty miles that way, got a ride back and went about twelve miles this way today," Fred said. He added that he wanted to hike another section shortly.

"I'll shuttle your car for you if you want me to," John offered.

That's another thing he does, shuttle hikers around to different parts of the trail. In his cluttered old car, he also keeps apples and oranges to pass out to fellow hikers, because "long-distance hikers are always hungry."

"I like to talk with the hikers," he said. "It's great fun."

Until 1974, John, a native of Illinois, never had been to the mountains. Then he was transferred to Roanoke from Norfolk with the gift company for which he was working. Later, he went to work for AT&T, and in the fall of 1985, he was transferred to Miami. He found himself longing for the mountains and the Appalachian Trail. He came back to visit and hike whenever he got the chance.

A year earlier, he had lost his job in cutbacks, and he returned to Rocky Mount, Virginia, about halfway between Roanoke and Martinsville.

"Nobody can ever entice me out of the mountains again," he said. "I just like being out here with the trees and the flowers and seeing the deer. I go at my own pace. I like to stop and look at wild flowers. Sometimes you find a place you just want to sit and enjoy. I just find it very relaxing. My wife used to say on weekends that I didn't go hiking that I was harder to get along with."

So far, John said, he'd hiked maybe a fourth of the trail at different times, but like many people who love it, he dreamed of doing the whole thing.

"Oh yes, that's one of my ambitions. Most likely it will occur after I retire. I know a guy who's hiked it seven times. He hiked it once in sixth-seven days. That's two-thousand, one-hundred miles in sixty-seven days. Imagine that."

A mile and a half past the point where I had left John sitting on the side of the road by his cluttered car, waiting to help other hikers, I came to the first tunnel along the parkway, passing through a ridge on the side of Bluff Mountain. I waited on the side of the road at the tunnel's entrance, enjoying the cool, damp breeze coming through it, until I could hear no traffic coming in either direction. Then I turned on the headlamp I had installed on my handlebars, the first time I'd had a chance to use it, and pedaled into the natural air conditioning. The tunnel was only 630 feet long, and the ride was short, the relief brief.

After a final brief ascent at Mile Post 56, this day's ride was downhill for the rest of the way. Soon Otter Creek was racing alongside the roadway, toward the flats less than a mile away. After entering the flats, the stream broadened and became less forceful and certain of its route, switching back and forth from one side of the parkway to the other.

I passed a big picnic area where somebody was cooking steaks over a charcoal fire, and the aroma stirred my hunger. I had to peddle now, but the going was easy. I passed the campground and coffee shop where I'd had lunch, a lake where water was coursing over the stone dam. A family of four was hiking along the lakeside trail.

Shortly, the James River Bridge appeared, and Linda was waiting for me at the visitor center. I had made nearly 37 miles this day, seven miles more than the average I had hoped to achieve and nearly 10 miles more than I'd made the first day. I wasn't all that tired either, and I felt good about the trip. But I knew that probably the biggest challenge of all awaited me tomorrow.

Trip Progress Log, Day Two: 37 miles
64 total miles completed, 405 to go.

DAY THREE

George Washington became so entranced with the James River that it flowed right into his dreams. From the time he first surveyed his way across Virginia, the man who would become our country's first president talked of connecting populous eastern Virginia to the West, where the country's future lay, by means of a canal along the James River, across the Blue Ridge Mountains and the continental divide, then down the Kanawha River to the Ohio.

In 1784, he finally set forth his plan to do just that.

The James River Company was formed to make the river navigable and Washington was elected its first president. He didn't live to see his vision become reality, however, for the simple reason that the undertaking proved to be so difficult that the first section of the canal, from Richmond to Lynchburg, wasn't completed until 1840, 41 years after Washington's death. The second stretch, from Lynchburg across the Blue Ridge to Buchanan, just 49 miles, wasn't finished until 1851.

Long narrow barges and packet boats pulled by draft horses ferried cargo and passengers along the canal for only a few years, however, before the steam engine and the coming of the railroad rendered Washington's dream obsolete.

That dream offered me an opportunity to delay facing the first real challenge to my own dream of conquering the Blue Ridge, although my dream was much more modest than Washington's. Naturally, I seized it.

I left my bike on the back of the car after arriving to start the third day of my ride, and Linda and I dawdled at the visitor center on the north bank of the James learning all about Washington's dream. On the far bank of the river, where a railroad now follows the old path of the

RESTORED LOCK: The National Park Service has restored one of the origi-
nal locks on the James River Canal.

canal, the Park Service had restored one of the canal's original locks
and diverted river water through it, and we strolled leisurely along the
foot bridge attached to the bottom of the highway bridge that carries
the parkway across the river to take a look at it.

All of this was self-defeating, of course, for it was going to be an
extremely hot day, the temperature already in the mid-80s at mid-
morning, predicted to climb into the 90s by noon. I only was making it
harder on myself the longer I waited to start up Apple Orchard Moun-
tain, one of the most dramatic ascents along the entire parkway.

It was almost 11:00 before I finally straddled my bike and struck
out across the Harry F. Byrd Memorial Bridge, the last flat stretch of
highway I would see for quite some time. Linda was planning to drive
on ahead to the lodge where we would spend the night, then return to
the first overlook to wait for me in case I keeled over from a heart
attack or heat exhaustion. That overlook was only seven and a half
miles away, but 1,700 feet higher. The James River Bridge marked the
lowest spot on the parkway, just 655 feet above sea level. Before the
day was out, I would have to climb to the parkway's highest point in
Virginia, 3,950 feet. In just 13 miles, I would be ascending 3,300 feet.

After a mile and a half I already was sweating heavily, and after
two miles I pulled into a shady spot to catch my breath, remove my

shirt and gulp some Gatorade. A sparrow hawk watched from the limb of an oak tree only 50 feet away.

Twenty minutes after leaving the James River, I had made only two and a half miles and my whole body was dripping with sweat. I kept slapping at big green-head flies that darted about me, zooming in at every opportunity to take stinging bites from my hide.

By the time I had entered the Jefferson National Forest, through which I would be riding for the next 35 miles, a breeze was stirring and I stopped to let it cool me. I stopped again at Mile Post 68, because the mile post itself was a curiosity. The squat concrete marker was set in a small spring. The water boiled up around it and trickled off down the mountainside. Wild strawberries were ripe here, and I abandoned my bike to pick a handful, sweet and wonderful.

Soon after I had left the wet-footed marker and the strawberries behind, a view opened so that I could see the parkway cutting through the rock of the mountainside high above. The spot was hardly a thousand yards away across a cove, but I would have to ride several miles to get there. It was a discouraging sight and an even more discouraging thought, and I tried to put it out of mind.

Near Mile Post 69, I came across two dead snakes in the road, only a few feet apart, and I stopped to examine one, because it was unlike any snake I'd ever seen, almost blue in color, but so badly smashed that I could tell little about it. The other was a common green snake. A half mile farther on, I came upon a buzzard, ugly and guilty looking, finishing the last morsels of another road kill. The big vulture lifted heavily into the air at my approach, leaving behind only a small brownish spot of blood and fat to mark the passage of whatever tiny creature had been its lunch.

Just past Mile Post 70, halfway to the top, I spotted another big patch of wild strawberries, excuse enough for a rest stop. Some of these were the biggest wild strawberries I'd ever seen, and I returned to the road with my palate sweetened and my hands stained red with juice.

The temperature surely had reached 90 now, and the climb was so strenuous that I felt myself overheating again after only half a mile or so. Conveniently, I came upon a spring pouring from a big rock, a natural, ever-running faucet of cold, crystal-clear water. While I doused my head under it, I could hear an owl hooting grumpily somewhere up the mountain, no doubt awakened by the heat.

I saw our car parked at the overlook as I approached Petite's Gap. Linda was resting nearby in the shade, reading a T.R. Pearson novel. She saw me coming and had a cold soft drink open and waiting by the time I got there.

"I was about to come looking for you," she said.

"Actually, I'm doing all right," I said. "The heat's what makes it so tough, but I think I'm going to make it."

I'd had a late breakfast, wasn't quite ready for lunch, and I decided to make it to the next overlook, two and a half miles away, before taking a break. Linda went on ahead, and as I was pushing off again, a familiar face appeared from a path leading to the Appalachian Trail: Fred Pittman, the hiker I'd met the day before when I'd stopped to talk with John Goodhart. He waved and I stopped to chat. He'd been making about as good time on foot, I learned, as I had on wheels.

Only a few minutes later, I broke out onto the ridge that I had spotted earlier, far below, when I had thought that I might never make it this far. Even from this vantage, it was an impressive accomplishment. The view here was grand, with the exception of a single smokestack spewing filth into the hazy horizon of the distant lowlands.

It was about 1:30 when I arrived at the Terrapin Mountain Overlook and found Linda ready for lunch. I had ridden only nine miles in two and a half hours, but I had climbed nearly half a mile. I had only another thousand feet to climb, and I was confident that I would make it now. A nice lunch and a short rest, and I would zip right over the top. I loaded the bike onto the back of the car and we drove on across the mountain to the lodge at Peaks of Otter, where we could have lunch in a lakeside dining room.

When Linda brought me back later to complete the day's ride, I told her to go on back to the lodge. The worst was behind me and there was no need for her to wait at the top to see if I would make it.

Half an hour later, I was wondering why I had told her that. Lunch and the short rest afterward apparently had drained my energy instead of replenishing it. Although it was cooler here than at the lower altitudes and there was a breeze coming down the mountainside, the late afternoon heat seemed to hang even heavier and more oppressively. But I had less than two miles of uphill left and I was determined to push on.

Soon after a brief stop at Thunder Ridge Overlook, butterflies pushed the heat out of my mind. Hundreds of dead and dying butterflies littered the roadway. They were black with blue, sienna and white spots. One banged into my helmet before fluttering to the pavement. I couldn't figure out what was happening. Had heat stricken some huge flight of butterflies? Had they simply strayed into the traffic at this high elevation? Was this section of the parkway built through some ancient butterfly dying ground?

I still was seeing dead and dying butterflies when I broke onto a ridge with a western view. All day I had been seeing only eastern views. Another helpful parkway sign told me that I was seeing Arnold's Valley but it was barely visible in the haze below, and there was only the faintest outline of the Allegheny Mountains across the valley. A groundhog was waiting to greet me as I approached the overlook. He sat on his haunches watching as I struggled toward him, confident that in my condition I was no threat, but as I grew nearer, he became less certain and scampered down the hillside.

The mountain rising over the valley to my right had two huge gaping wounds in its forested side, one a broad, reddish mudslide near the base that had carried away everything in its path, the other a gigantic rockslide near the summit that had left the mountain's gray, granite innards exposed, vivid evidence that these venerable mountains are ever changing.

Soon after leaving the overlook, I came around a sharp curve and caught a glimpse of the gleaming radar dome that dominates the peak of Apple Orchard Mountain. Once part of a Nike missile site, it now serves a more useful purpose, directing traffic into Washington airports. My goal was in sight, and I was homing in on it with the intensity of a radar beam. I was bucking a stiff headwind as I passed Mile Post 76, just over half a mile from the top, requiring greater exertion but cooling me for my extra effort.

The summit was just ahead, a tenth of a mile or so, and I was tempted to pedal on toward it in triumph, but the overlook came first, with a view to the east and northeast and an exhibit explaining how Apple Orchard Mountain got its name: "Wind, ice and snow of racing winter storms have pruned this mountaintop forest, giving it an old apple orchard appearance. This 'orchard' consists primarily of gnarled, lichen-covered northern red oak." Yet right by the sign was a maple and several other non-oak varieties.

The ride to the top was so easy that I sprinted across it.

"Well, I licked you, you big mother," I said to the mountain.

It had taken me an hour and five minutes to make those last four miles, but I knew now that I had passed the parkway's test. Barring accident or other unforeseen difficulties, I would make it to the end, and I was jubilant as I started down the mountain's southern slope.

The next nine miles would pass in a third of the time that it had taken me to complete the last stage of my climb to the top. I dropped 500 feet in about three minutes, braking numerous times to prevent my speed from building to dangerous levels. After a short incline, I descended another 300 feet in a single mile. But as is to be expected along the parkway, I soon had to go up again to continue downward. This climb lasted for only about half a mile, before I was racing downhill once more.

I paused at the parking area for the trail leading to Falling Water Cascades. I could hear the cascades half a mile away but opted not to take the hike to see them. It was a fortuitous decision, for if I had done so, I would have missed a wondrous sight, something I'd never seen before.

Only moments after leaving the parking area, racing downhill again, I saw a huge bird flying down the middle of the parkway straight toward me at about head height. It veered upward and to my right as we passed and I saw its zebra-striped head and big crest, as brilliantly red as my own helmet, and I recognized it immediately from my bird book: a pileated woodpecker. I stopped and turned back, hoping to catch another glimpse of it, but it had disappeared into the trees.

I faced only one more uphill stretch before I rolled happily into the high valley of Peaks of Otter, which has been a popular stopover for travelers for more than a century and a half. Here still stands the cabin that was Polly Woods Ordinary, where Polly, a widow, provided the ordinary needs of travelers, a bed and meals, from 1834 until 1859. Benjamin Wilkes built a hotel in the valley in 1849 that was expanded after World War I and renamed the Mons Hotel, becoming a popular resort until it burned in 1941.

Now the rustic Peaks of Otter Lodge nestles by a big reflective lake under the three mountains that form the Peaks of Otter – Flat Top, Sharp Top and Harkening Hill. The lodge, near the site where Polly Woods' cabin still stands, would be my resting place for the night.

As Linda and I sat in the dining room later, looking out at Abbot Lake and Sharp Top, a cone-shaped mountain with a pointed peak of bare stone that gives it an almost mystical quality, I couldn't help but

GRAND REFLECTION: Sharp Top Mountain reflects in Abbot Lake at the Peaks of Otter.

think about a book I had written about a series of murders. One of the murder missions had originated at the Park Service campground at the base of Sharp Top. Under the waters of Abbot Lake, I knew, was a part of the pistol that had been used to shoot the three victims. Somewhere nearby was buried the heavy hunting knife that had been used to slit their throats. Not exactly pleasant thoughts for dinner. But there would be a more pleasant experience to close this hard but heartening day.

At twilight, Linda and I went for a walk to a restored farm set on the side of Harkening Hill a mile from the lodge. As we entered a meadow of high grass and wild flowers near the parkway, a deer stood grazing not a hundred feet away. It turned to look at us but didn't bolt. It simply watched us pass and returned to its supper. We took a different, wooded trail back to the lodge and startled two more deer at a spring, a doe and a young buck. They fled through the trees and across a ridge, their white tails flared in alert.

Trip Progress Log, Day Three: 22 miles
86 total miles completed, 383 to go.

DAY FOUR

Linda had become interested in the wild flowers along the parkway, which were everywhere in great profusion, and we had bought a book so that we could identify and learn about them. I had been browsing through the book at night, searching out some of the flowers I had been seeing on my ride, and already I could identify quite a few by sight.

As I began the fourth day of my ride, from the parking lot at Peaks of Otter Lodge, I picked out wild cranesbill, crested iris, May apple and painted trillium within the first half mile. I also took note of several others that I'd have to look up later.

Just after passing the gas station at the Peaks of Otter Recreation Area, my search for wild flowers was interrupted by a movement on the pavement directly in front of my bike. A small garter snake, maybe 14 inches long, slithered into my path and I had to swerve off the roadway to keep from running over it. I'd already done in one big beetle and a butterfly on my ride and I didn't want to take another creature's life. Startled by my sudden movement, the snake coiled and remained in place, and I had to turn back and prod it to get it off the pavement to safety.

I had a quick three-mile downhill run to Powell's Gap, once a passageway through the mountains for great herds of lumbering buffalo, but the only sign of the presence of any creature here now was the strong odor of a skunk that was not to be seen.

Climbing again, breathing hard, I took note of more wild flowers, sunflowers, columbine, daisies, golden rod, wild roses, and several little flowers in varying shades of purple that I couldn't recognize. At the Porter's Mountain Overlook, I paused to study an exhibit about oak trees, set appropriately beneath five big oaks, all of different species.

"The oaks rank with the world's most important trees," I read, "furnishing fine lumber for man and food for many species of wildlife. Venerated by ancient people, oaks are still regarded as symbols of strength."

Although not quite ancient yet, I thought highly of oaks, too, and I was immensely pleased with myself that I could identify all five species before me without help from the exhibit.

But tied around one of the oaks was a disturbing sight, a green insect trap installed by the U.S. Forest Service with warnings not to molest it – the first sign I had seen of the southward advance of the forest-destroying gypsy moth.

After another short breather at Bear Wallow Gap, I started up an incline steep enough to make me realize that my legs had been considerably weakened by their effort of the day before. After breaking onto a ridge that would, if not for a stand of sumac on my left, have offered views off each side, I came to the Purgatory Mountain Overlook. Laurel was blooming here, and I paused to peruse an exhibit on hawks.

The next overlook offered another crossing of the Appalachian Trail and a fine view back at Sharp Top, from which I had come, just over six miles away. It seemed farther, somehow, in the haze and heat. Two miles farther along, it had all but disappeared.

The breeze had died, making the heat nearly unbearable, and I was sweating so much that I had emptied my Gatorade and started on my water bottle, occasionally removing my helmet and pouring a little over my head. The changes in altitude were only a few hundred feet, but there were plenty of them. I stopped for a view of the town of Montvale in the Goose Creek Valley, then pedaled on to the Taylor's Mountain Overlook, where I stopped in a coughing fit, gagging on a bug that had flown into my mouth.

Two miles farther on, I stopped out of sheer wonder. A steep rock face rose along the right side of the parkway, and about 15 feet up its side, growing from a tiny crevice, was a peach tree with small green peaches on it. I had planted 16 peach trees at home years ago, and despite better soil, a far better climate for peaches and hours of pruning and spraying, I'd never gotten even a single peach. Yet here were peaches growing wild in the harshest of conditions. Go figure.

A breeze was stirring now, and on it came an amazing puff ball, as big as a softball, tumbling down the parkway, as I approached an overlook offering a spectacular view of the Great Valley stretching between the Blue Ridge and the Alleghenies. As I was enjoying the sight, a fellow approached to chat. Another visitor from England. He was spending three weeks driving from Atlanta to Washington, and had chosen to follow the parkway for much of that distance. Never, he said, had he seen such a lovely road. He seemed a bit morose that his journey soon would be coming to an end.

I was headed down now, and the views were less beautiful: a huge quarry, power lines, a railroad. I was approaching the first city along the parkway's route, and just past Mile Post 104, I encountered a subdivision fast by the parkway, neat little ranch houses standing in rows.

There would be only more of these signs of civilization as the parkway skirted Roanoke. Not only would there be more sub-divisions crowding the parkway along the next 15 miles, but the views, when there were any, would be mainly of hillside suburbs and apartment complexes. The parkway became thick with impatient and speeding commuters. Litter, relatively rare along the parkway, became more obvious. At one overlook, a pair of lavender bikini panties decorated a split-rail fence.

I was pleased to leave all of this behind and pull into the Ranger Station near Vinton for a meeting I'd previously arranged with two part-time rangers, Mosie Reid and Ajena Cason. They greeted me warmly, and we sat outside at a picnic table to talk.

When she moved to the mountains in 1983, Mosie told me, she felt instantly at home.

Even though she had been born and reared in Silver Spring, Maryland, a suburb of Washington, she knew that mountain blood flowed in her veins because it set the beat for the mountain music that she sang and played so naturally on guitar and mandolin.

Years earlier, her mother's family had migrated to the Washington area from a steel mill town in eastern Ohio, and in the neighborhood where Mosie grew up were many other families who had done the same thing, many of them coming from the mountains of West Virginia and Virginia.

"Everybody just played music there," Mosie told me. "I've been picking music all my life. My brothers play. Mom plays."

Music led her frequently to the mountains to attend fiddling conventions and bluegrass festivals. And after she married a bluegrass musician and record producer from Maryland, it led her to the mountains to live. Although she later separated from her husband, she remained in the mountains, and in the newspaper she kept seeing notices about the campfire programs at the Roanoke Mountain campground on the Blue Ridge Parkway.

One day in 1984, Mosie walked into the ranger station near Vinton and offered herself as a volunteer to do campfire programs. Soon she was volunteering 30 hours a week and more. One of the programs she wanted to present was on the roots of mountain music. She got three other musicians to join her, and they started performing at the campground every Sunday night. Word got around, and the crowds grew steadily bigger.

"Next year, they had a job open," Mosie said of the park service, "and they said, would I like it, and I said I'd love it."

It was just a summer job, but that suited Mosie fine. By then she had become a student at Radford College, had taken some Appalachian studies courses and had become interested in the lives of mountain women in earlier times. She had been impressed that women she had met in the mountains were little different than those she had known growing up.

"So many of the things that they would say, the expressions they would use, the things they would do when their kids were sick were so similar," she said.

She began reading a lot about mountain people, particularly books by mountain women. Mountain people, she knew, had been stereotyped, and she wanted to do something to correct that.

"There's always that impression that mountain people were dumb, that the things they did were out of ignorance," she said. "What I wanted to reflect was their ingenuity. There is a resourcefulness, and if you just look a little beyond, you can understand what may seem strange."

But getting across her point at campfire programs, she discovered, was not easy.

"I felt like I was lecturing people," she said. "You know, you have something you really want to say and you can't get it across. You can't just stand up here and say this is true and that's not true."

She wanted something more personal, more vivid, and she came up with the idea of a little one-person play, set in the half century between 1880 and 1930. Mosie would portray a mountain woman at three different stages of her life – newly married, after having several children, and as an old woman. To set the mood, she would play mandolin and sing old mountain ballads, also using the music as transitions between

PERFORMING DUO: Mosie Reid, left, and Ajena Cason give performances of mountain women at campfire circles along the parkway.

the changes. She spent weeks researching and writing her parts and preparing her costumes.

"It's just designed to give some factual content but to help people to recognize the diversity of skills needed to just survive from day to day and the impacts that – say, World War I and the coming of industry and the Blue Ridge Parkway – had on people here, just the outside world and how it changed things.

When she had it all together, she tried it all out on her friend Ajena Cason.

Ajena had been born in Roanoke, had grown up near the mountains, and she had been recommended for a summer job with the park service after finishing her first year as a physics major at Radford. She encouraged Mosie. And after Mosie's character became a popular success at campfire circles, Mosie began talking to Ajena about creating a similar character of her own, but one with a different perspective.

"People don't look at black people as being Appalachian people," Mosie said, "but they are. The blacks just kept to themselves in these areas. When people were writing about the mountain folks, they just didn't see them. Blacks had a big influence on mountain culture – spiritually, musically and in other ways, yet they're often ignored, so we felt that we had to do something about that."

Ajena created her own character, Granny Foster, an old mountain black woman looking back on her life.

"It just fell together," she said. "Most of it I picked up from people around me, especially my grandmother and the older ladies at my church."

Usually, Mosie and Ajena do their characters individually at campfire circles. But occasionally they have performed together. Both told me that they hoped to become full-time rangers so they can keep dispelling stereotypes and showing people what life once was like for mountain women, both black and white.

"We love it," said Mosie. "I try to never think of it as a performance but as a sharing."

Alas, neither would be presenting their programs so that I could see them on this trip, but I would try to come back, I promised, when they would be performing.

The ride was mostly downhill from the ranger station to the Roanoke River, which slices through a deep, rocky gorge 165 feet beneath the bridge on which the parkway crosses it. This bridge holds two distinctions: It is the highest along the parkway and it is the favored spot along the parkway for suicides.

"We average about one or two a year there," a ranger at the Vinton station had told me.

The view from the bridge prompts many to people walk onto it and photograph it. Linda was waiting for me here, and we followed a trail along rocky cliffs to an overlook that not only offers a better view of the river but of the bridge as well.

It was 91 degrees according to the car radio, when I got back on my bike to begin the climb. By the time I had reached a steep, four-mile, one-way spur of the parkway that leads to the top of Roanoke Mountain, I knew that I did not want to take any steep-climb side trips. Instead, I took a much shorter downhill spur road to Mill Mountain Park, where Linda was waiting for me again. Here is a campground, picnic area, zoo – and the "world's biggest star," a huge five-pointed neon sign mounted on steel girders that shines over Roanoke every night, symbolizing its self-proclaimed status as the "star city" of the South.

The view of the bustling city with its traffic-clogged arteries is spectacular – and enough to make a tired bicyclist happy to be back on the parkway for the quick one-mile downhill run to U.S. 220 and the end of another day's ride.

Trip Progress Log, Day Four: 35 miles
121 total miles completed, 348 to go.

DAY FIVE

The fifth day of my ride began not on the parkway but in a super-market deli in Roanoke, where Linda and I shopped for the ingredients of a picnic lunch: smoked turkey, kaiser rolls, German potato salad, kosher pickles, cheese and fruit and puff pastries. No more Beanee-Weenee picnics.

Linda dropped me off at my starting spot, and went on up the park-way to prepare our picnic. A front had passed through during the night, dropping temperatures considerably, and the riding promised to be pleasant if the rain held off. But ominous black clouds hovered around the distant peaks.

Eight miles and nearly 1,000 feet in altitude later, the sun was shin-ing brightly when I wheeled into the Poages Mill Overlook, where Linda was waiting with our picnic spread on a blanket. We ate looking down at the city of Roanoke, a toy town now in the distance.

Another 1,000 feet of climbing awaited me after lunch, and this time over a much shorter distance. Just two miles ahead lay the steep-est grade on the parkway southbound, four degrees. A mile and a half into the grade, I was breathing hard and getting hot under the rain suit I had donned, for the sky was now totally black, the wind whipping tiny droplets of rain. But after only another mile and a half, the rain had dis-appeared and the sun was once again shining through the clouds.

At Slings Gap, I put steep climbing behind me for a while. This was the portal to the Blue Ridge Plateau, a 170-mile stretch of moun-taintop pastures, farm fields and wooded hillsides, with few drastic changes in elevation. For the next six days, the riding rarely would be difficult.

Just past the view of Poor Mountain, a hay field brought me a

GOOD FOR A LAUGH: Some practical jokester farmer had done his own sculpture in this hayfield.

laugh. The field was vast and dotted with big rolls of freshly mown hay. From the center of one roll close by the roadside a pair of blue-jeaned legs and booted feet protruded, a farmer's practical joke for passersby on the parkway.

A mile farther along, at Adney Gap, potato fields, deep green, lay along both sides of the parkway, giving way to vast fields of cabbage, blue-green and luminescent. Another mile and the woods were deep, lined with banks of flame azaleas in several shades of orange and yellow. Not all was beauty, however, for a few miles farther on I came upon a house with at least a dozen junked cars spread around it. But soon I was at the view of the Devil's Backbone, and it was a magnificent one indeed, of big white farm houses, silos and lush fields.

At the Pine Spur Overlook, I came upon a small mystery. A hearse, a limousine and a funeral home flower wagon were parked here, but no one was around. Small family cemeteries are common along the parkway (many lie on parkway land), but none was in sight at this spot.

I rode on past more farm fields, a farmer mowing hay, cows pausing in their grazing to watch me pass. Just past Mile Post 147, a farmer's angry dog chased after me, nipping at my heels as I pedaled furiously, soon outdistancing him. The hard pedaling caused my right leg to cramp, and I had to stop a mile farther on to work it out.

I dreaded one spot that was coming up, the site of the fatal motorcycle wreck we had come upon in our scouting trip. The reminders were still there: broken glass in the ditch, the skid marks, stains from fuel and blood, paint marks where the bodies had been. I was thankful to get past it and on to more pleasant views.

Just past Mile Post 153, I stopped at a neat brick house on a slight rise overlooking the parkway. A man was working in his garden. His name was Jessie Sutphin, and I knew about him. We soon were seated at his kitchen table, looking at old photographs he had brought out.

In one of the photos, a group of men stood in rows, posing proudly in winter uniform. Jessie went down the ranks, calling some by name, others by reputation, offering observations.

"This boy, he got killed out in Grand Canyon...This was my district ranger...This little feller here, he killed hisself...Here's our chief ranger. He was a hell of a nice somebody...That was the whole group, twenty-eight men. I would say it was the first ranger meeting that they had."

· Jessie was in the photo, too, still a young man, proud and happy to be a warden on the Blue Ridge Parkway, soon to be a ranger. He admits that he may have been the proudest and happiest ranger ever to work for the National Park Service. His wife, Agnes, told me that nobody ever loved his job or the parkway more.

Jessie first came to the parkway in 1947 at age 29. He'd been married for a year and a half, and he wasn't happy with his work.

"I had several jobs in Roanoke that a dog wouldn't have," he recalled. "I told my wife, 'I'm going to buy me a little farm. We may not have much money, but we'll have plenty to eat,' and I came back and bought this little place here."

This little place was 53 acres that had belonged to his wife's grandmother. It lay alongside the parkway, which had opened a few years before. People told Jessie that he wouldn't be able to grow grass on the place, but he cleared a hillside and proved them wrong. He raised cattle and vegetables and found the peace his soul and troubled stomach needed.

Jessie was reared on a farm near Salem, Virginia, but he left at 16 to join the Civilian Conservation Corps. He worked in several CCC camps and helped build Hanging Rock State Park near Danbury, North Carolina before joining the Army in 1939.

PARKWAY MAN: Retired ranger Jessie Sutphin and his wife, Agnes, in front of their home on the parkway.

The outbreak of World War II took Jessie to Europe, He served in three invasions – North Africa, Sicily and Normandy – and 15 major battles as a combat medic. "Normandy," he says,"was where I waded in blood to get to dry land." He was pushing into Germany when his stomach began bothering him so much that he was hospitalized. The condition, doctors decided, was due to combat stress, and it led to his reassignment and discharge in 1945. He returned home, married and took the jobs that brought him to his farm and the parkway.

A few years after he got his farm going, Jessie volunteered to fight a forest fire that had spread to parkway land from a neighbor's brush fire. Afterwards, the district ranger asked if he'd be interested in a job. Jessie said that he would, and he soon was made a park warden. The pay was $2,400 a year.

"At that time, it was a whole lot of money, you know, and I was proud," he said.

Five years later, he was a ranger – and even prouder. He worked hard to promote good feeling between local people and the Park Service. He visited with them, cleared their roads of snow in winter. He could be firm with those who caused trouble along the parkway, but he knew he was respected for the manner in which he handled matters.

Once, for example, he was lauded for the way he dealt with a local teenager he had caught driving recklessly, squealing his tires and leaving marks on the parkway.

"I took his little butt in," he recalled, "and the judge, Judge Charles B. Fox Jr., asked me what I thought ought to be done with him. He was good to ask me what I thought. I said, 'Well, he left all those tire marks. I'd like for him to go up there and scrub 'em off.'"

The judge pronounced just that sentence, and a photograph of the young man on his hands and knees trying to remove the marks with a brush appeared in newspapers all over the country.

"By golly, he done it, too," Jessie recalled with a laugh.

Jessie's wife grew accustomed to him bringing stranded parkway travelers to their home for a meal, or even for a night. She knew, too, that wasn't all he did for strangers.

"People'd run out of gas and not have any money," Jessie recalled. "I'd give 'em five dollars and say, 'Send it back to me.' Know how many of those five dollars I ever got? None."

Yet that never stopped him from helping the next stranded visitor. It was part of the job, he figured.

"That was the love I had for it, you see. If there's any enjoyment in anything I ever done, I enjoyed every hour of it."

"He worshipped his job," his wife added. "That's probably why he lost it."

After more than 20 years of happy service, Jessie got a new supervisor who, he said, offended him the first day, later treated him with disrespect and made his life so difficult that he no longer could enjoy his work.

"My stomach got to going back to what it was in the war," he said.

Doctors told him that he had to get away from the source of his trouble, and in 1974, after 23 years with the park service, he took disability retirement.

It didn't work. He was miserable away from his job. His stomach troubles continued, and his anger and bitterness grew.

"Last fifteen years, I've lived through hell," he said.

When he first retired, Jessie asked his wife to take down some curtains so that he could sit in his favorite chair and look out onto the parkway, but now he avoids the road he once loved so deeply.

"I go down here two miles and cut off, or I go down to (highway) 860 and cut off, get the hell off of it," he told me.

Yet if he could have changed things, he said, there was no doubt what he'd have done. He'd have remained a parkway ranger.

"I'd've been out there today," he said. "Yeah boy. Yeah boy."

Trip Progress Log, Day Five: 34 miles
155 total miles completed, 314 to go.

DAY SIX

Day Six was a perfect day for bike riding: clear and breezy, the sky a deep blue, the temperature only in the 60s as I left Smart View Recreation Area, which offers a 19th century log cabin, a picnic area, restrooms and hiking trails. The riding was easy, and traffic was light.

I passed a farmer baling hay, a pasture filled with red-wing blackbirds, a church with blue windows, a vine-entwined old cabin with a crumbling stone chimney, an expansive field of winter wheat already turning yellow, soon to be ready for harvest, a crystal clear mill pond, the mill itself long gone.

I had made nine miles in the first hour, despite several stops, and was feeling very good about the world, when a black van suddenly came up in a rush behind me and swerved deliberately toward me, a young man hanging from the passenger window whooping and beating on the door. I swerved off the pavement and managed to come to a safe stop, as the van disappeared around a curve. I'd had things like this happen while I was riding in other places, but this was the first such incident on the parkway, and it depressed me more than angering me.

I'd managed to put it behind me by the time I'd passed Tuggle's Gap. Only a short distance beyond, I saw a movie camera mounted on a tripod near a clump of laurel, and a young man suddenly appeared from behind a bush, running across the field toward me waving his arms. I stopped to see what he wanted, and he explained that he was from a California film production company, making a documentary about the parkway. He wanted to get a shot of a bicyclist coming across the ridge with the split-rail fence in the background, and he was not ready when I came across. Would I mind going back and riding by again so that he could get the shot?

MOUNTAINTOP VISTA: A view from The Saddle, a windswept ridge at Rocky Knob.

I was happy to oblige, amused that I had pedaled myself right into a movie. He gave me a signal to start, and when I'd ridden out of camera range, I returned to see if he'd gotten the shot. He had, he said, but would I mind doing it once more so that he could be sure? I repeated my performance, and when I went back this time to make sure I'd done okay, I quizzed him a little.

He'd been working on the film for only a couple of weeks, he said, and it was his first visit to the parkway. He was from Arizona. Tucson. And this was entirely different country from any he'd ever known.

The parkway was more beautiful than he'd imagined, he said, but until the day before, he'd been getting very discouraged. The heat had been so intense as to make his work miserable. The haze of pollution that had been hanging over the mountains had kept him from getting good shots of the more spectacular views. He'd gotten scraped and bug-bitten crawling around trying to get shots of wild flowers and little creatures. But then the front had come through, the air had cleared, the temperature had dropped and the parkway had become a completely different place than it had been just the day before. He was working overtime now, he said, rushing to get as many shots as he could while the weather was so beautiful. I didn't want to hold him up any longer, wished him well and left him to his work.

All beauty comes with a price, and I was about to pay mine for the day, a three-mile climb of 600 feet to the Rocky Knob Recreation Area, a network of campgrounds, cabins, picnic areas, and some of the best hiking trails along the parkway. My reward came as soon as I turned off the parkway and climbed the hill to the parking area known as the Saddle, a windswept ridge that offers views of breath-taking beauty in every direction, including a good look at a long stretch of the parkway over which I'd just ridden. I recognized the field where the film maker had been.

Less than a mile away, Rocky Knob provided two more spectacular views of Rock Castle Gorge below, so named because of its deposits of quartz crystals shaped like the turrets of medieval castles, and the peach-growing region beyond.

Linda was waiting for me at Morrisette Winery, a big stone building just off the parkway with a fine restaurant and a big bar for sampling the winery's several varieties. It was a little early in the day for wine tasting, but I tried a Seyval Blanc and Merlot anyway, both newly issued, both quite appealing.

Linda drove on ahead as I rode downhill at a fast clip through a sweeping turn past the distant vineyards. Within minutes I had reached the most congested spot on the parkway, where the speed limit dropped from 45 to 25, and a rare sight for the parkway appeared: no parking signs.

Mabry Mill at Mile Post 172 is said to be the most photographed scene along the parkway, one of the most photographed scenes in the whole country, and it must be true, for as I rode up, several people were busy taking pictures of it. So popular is the mill that it's the only place on the parkway with overflow parking lots. And on any weekend day in summer and fall, those parking lots likely will be filled, as they were this day. On some days, even the overflow lots are overflowing.

"This ain't nothin' to what it will be," Wendell Sutphin told me several minutes later. He was eating a sausage biscuit on his lunch break and watching a steady line of curious tourists traipse through the dusty mill. Nearby, Ray Barlow, a big man in overalls, an apprentice miller, was showing off a handful of buckwheat seeds.

"Actually, it's not related to wheat," he was saying. "It's more of an herb. Used to be a lot of buckwheat grown in this part of the country."

PHOTOGENIC SPOT: Mabry Mill is said to be the most photographed scene on the parkway.

Uncle Ed Mabry and his wife, Lizzie, whom he called Boss, moved into a two-room cabin on this spot in 1899, and during the next few years Uncle Ed built a small industrial complex – a blacksmith shop, a sawmill and gristmill. Because he had chosen such a level spot, he had to build a pond and an elaborate series of flumes to provide the water needed to turn the mill's wheel and create its power.

That wheel, reconstructed after the deaths of the Mabrys more than half a century earlier, turned with a comforting rhythm, as Wendell Sutphin, the miller for the past four years, finished his lunch. Earlier, he and Ray Barlow had ground a batch of cornmeal. They also grind grits and buckwheat flour to sell to the constant parade of visitors.

"Fall of the year, it's a sight," Wendell said. "You can't even get in here fall of the year. Be ten times this many comin' through this fall."

Nearby, at a cabin reconstructed on the site of the Mabry home, Frances Radford of Ararat, Virginia, wearing a long dress and bonnet, was carding wool, preparing to show a group of tourists how mountain women once spun it into yarn.

"This is sheep wool, a little dirty," she said, pausing to pick trash

SPINNING WHEEL: Frances Radford of Ararat, Virginia, spins yarn at Mabry Mill.

A MUSICAL BASH: Local musicians gather at Mabry Mill almost every week-end in summer and early fall, to play old mountain music on a variety of instruments.

from it. " A little dirtier than I care to use, but it's just an old barnyard animal."

She carefully explained every step as she transformed the wool to yarn on a wooden spinning wheel.

"How did you learn this?" somebody asked.

"I'd like to say from my grandmother," she said with a smile, "but I don't remember my grandmother doing this. Actually, I was taught by another ranger, who went to Berea College in Kentucky to learn it."

No ranger had to teach the musicians who were playing under a shed where molasses is made each fall. Local musicians gather here almost every weekend in summer and early fall, most of them middle-aged men and older, to play old mountain music on banjos, fiddles, guitars, mandolins and dulcimers, and always some in the audience are moved to do a little flat-foot dancing, as several couples were doing.

At the blacksmith shop behind the shed where the musicians were performing, Phipps Bourne had stepped outside for a cooling breath. Nobody would have guessed his name from the tag pinned on his blue work shirt. His name tag is unlike those worn by other rangers. Others

PARKWAY BLACKSMITH: Phipps Bourne, who is nicknamed "Festus," demonstrates blacksmithing skills. He also performs many other tasks along the parkway, including repairing fence rails, building exhibits and doing some wood carving.

tell first name and last. His offers only a nickname: Festus.

"After I started to work here, they couldn't remember my right name," he explained, "so they started calling me that."

No doubt it had something to do with his drawl, which makes him sound a lot like the character on the old TV show "Gunsmoke" who bore the same handle.

Never mind the unusual name tag, though. Phipps Bourne is a ranger who would be noticed anyway. For one thing, he is six feet five inches tall and usually dressed in farmer's garb. Beyond that, he is a man of diverse talents and keen country observations. (Of the media, he says: "A watchdog that barks at everything and bites anything in sight ain't much good.")

For the past 18 years, Festus, as he prefers to be called, has spent half of each year as a ranger on the parkway and the other half as a cattle farmer and craftsman on his 400 acres at Elk Creek in Grayson County, Virginia, about 14 miles west of Galax. "My people settled the valley in seventeen and sixty-six," he said, "and we've been there ever since."

His principal duty for the Park Service is to demonstrate blacksmithing skills, which he does five days a week in summer and fall. But he also does much more.

If fence rails or roofing shakes need to be replaced along the parkway, it's Festus who splits them with ancient hand tools. If old farm implements need to be fixed or restored, Festus does it. If some old device or odd item needs to be made for another national park, Festus often gets called upon. He made hinges for the home of the poet Carl Sandburg at Flat Rock, North Carolina He built moonshine stills for exhibits on the parkway and in Great Smoky Mountains National Park. He also presents parkway campfire programs on blacksmithing and woodworking.

"Later on," he said, "I may work up one on moonshinin'. That's one I don't feel as comfortable with 'cause I don't know much about it. I'll have to take the other feller's word fer that."

So how did he manage to build two stills with such limited experience?

"I done a little research before I started," he said with a sly grin. "And you'd be surprised when you start something like that how many people come around and give you some information."

Twice Festus has gone to Washington to demonstrate his skills at the Smithsonian Institute, once for blacksmithing, another time for wood carving. He carved figures of birds and animals as well as intricate ornamental pieces for antique furniture.

"I just carved mostly for fun," he said. "Then people got to wantin' things and it got to be work instead of enjoyment and I just finally quit."

Festus never had any training in blacksmithing and doesn't know where those skills came from. "Just born that way, I reckon. There never was a blacksmith in the family that I knew of. I guess you could say I'm the blacksmith in the family."

Necessity actually prompted him to take it up, he said.

"When you own a farm, they's a whole lot of stuff gets broke and bent and there wasn't anybody around to fix it and I just got to playing with it and learned some. That's one thing about blacksmithing: you can make your own mistakes instead of buying somebody else's.

"Mostly what I learned, I learnt here with everybody watching. I just take a notion to do something and go to it. That's the trouble with people nowadays; they've quit thinking. I just think up what I want to do and do it. If you're artistic enough to get it in your head, you can get it in your hands.

"The old blacksmith said, 'Just get it in your head what you want to make and then beat it to hell until it looks like it. If you're wood carvin', you just cut off everything that don't look like it.'"

Four miles from Mabry Mill, I was drawn inexorably toward another old building, this one a store facing a road parallel to the parkway. Maybe it was the authentic, old-time country look of the place that drew me. But unquestionably its name had something to do with it, too. Mayberry Trading Post.

Could this be the place where Andy Griffith got the name for the fictional town in his famous TV show?

"I'm confident that he did," said Addie Wood. "His mother was raised within seven miles of here, and Andy's father I know beyond doubt came to the store here and brought him when he was just a little boy. Andy's mother told me that."

The store is the center of activity for the tiny community of Mayberry, which is only about 25 miles up the mountain from Mount Airy, North Carolina, Andy's hometown.

"Been a store here I know as far back as eighteen and sixty," Addie told me.

FAMOUS NAME: The Mayberry Trading Post is four miles from Mabry Mill. Proprietor Addie Wood says Andy Griffith came to the store when he was a small child.

Not that she remembers that far back, of course. But at 86, she can remember going to the store when she was just a tiny girl. And for the past 21 years, she's been the storekeeper.

Before that, Addie cooked apple butter under a shed outside the store each fall – and it wasn't that weak, insipid swill some people try to pass off as apple butter nowadays, she emphasized. No sir.

"You've got to cook that stuff," she said emphatically. "You can't just take it off in two or three hours and call it apple butter. You have to cook apple butter seven or eight hours after you quit puttin' apples in to make real ol'-timey apple butter."

That may sound like a lot of hard work, but that was something Addie was accustomed to. She was born just a mile and a half from the store in the house where she still lives. Her father farmed 53 acres and after he died she did it herself.

"Just had to dig it out on the farm, winter and summer. I've done everything on a farm I reckon could be done with horses except run a mowin' machine. Just didn't have the nerve to get on a mowin' machine and hook a team to it and take out a-mowin'. I raked hay, stacked hay, hauled corn, raised lots of chickens, milked cows. I got by.

"I hear a lot of people talk about the good ol' days. They don't want to go back and live the way we used to live. They miss the hospitality, the way people used to visit and all, but they don't want to go out and live like we had to."

When farming got so it wasn't paying much, Addie looked for other ways to bring in a little money.

She started making molasses and apple butter nearly 40 years ago, first at Mabry Mill, then at the Mayberry Store, which Coy O. Yeatts ran for more than 35 years. The state of Virginia ran Coy Yeatts out of business by imposing a sales tax.

"When they put that state tax on him, he locked the door and walked out," Addie recalled. "Said he didn't want to deal with it, didn't want to charge people tax."

Later, Addie and Coy's son, Coy Lee, who married Addie's niece, became partners and reopened the store as a crafts shop for parkway visitors. Addie even made a few bonnets to sell. But local people kept coming in wanting grocery items, soft drinks and this-and-that, so the store went back to being a store with a lot of geegaws and gimcracks for tourists.

Now, locals and tourists gather at the back counter to eat pork-and-

SHOPKEEPER: Addie Wood, proprietor of the Mayberry Trading Post.

beans and sardines from cans, and sandwiches that they make themselves from ingredients Addie sells. And most of them try to get Addie to talking about the old days. She almost always obliges, telling stories about Simon, the tanner, or Ed Mabry, the miller, or about Andy Griffith's relatives, or how she had to gather chestnuts and sell them for three cents a pound and scrape and save to get a little pair of oxfords that she wanted as a teenager.

"Young people now I wonder what they'd do if they had to go out and scrape things like that," she said. "You can't get a child to even turn around for a dollar nowadays. It's pathetic.

"They ought to at least learn so if they have to work they know how."

One of the store regulars interrupted to point out that some of Addie's customers like to tease her about being an old maid.

"Yep," she admitted, "just strictly an old maid. Oh, I used to frolic around some in my teens and twenties. I say marriage is all right if you find the right one, but I believe it would be something else if you didn't. I never did find the right one."

She laughed and added an afterthought.

"I'm still lookin'."

Trip Progress Log, Day Six: 31 miles
186 total miles completed, 283 to go.

DAY SEVEN

The heat had returned, but the sky was clear and providing a good breeze as I started the climb up Groundhog Mountain, where no groundhogs were to be seen. What was to be seen in the picnic area at the top of the mountain was a log tower that once was used by the Virginia Forest Service. It had long ago been abandoned to tourists, and Linda and I joined several to climb to the top and enjoy a magnificent view of Pilot Mountain, rising regally from the lowlands far below, toward the city of Winston-Salem.

With its odd, knob pinnacle, Pilot is one of the most distinctive mountains in the country. Early settlers called it Ararat, possibly because in its isolated splendor it made them think of a spot where an ark might settle in a great flood. But Indians had earlier called the mountain The Great Guide, thus it became Pilot.

Beneath the tower was an exhibit of the beautiful rail fences that line so much of the parkway. In my research through Park Service statistics, I had learned that the parkway has 1,642,467 linear feet of rail fencing, using 861,401 rails (don't ask me who counted them). The rails came from the American chestnut trees that once covered the mountains but were killed in a blight during the 1920s, offering a ready source of easy-to-split, durable wood to be turned into rails.

The exhibit offered me a chance to learn about the different types of fences I had been seeing on my ride. There were, I discovered, four basic types: snake, buck, stake-and-rider, and post-and-rail.

Snake fences are simply rails piled atop one another in a zig-zag pattern. The stake-and-rider is similar to the snake but has posts where the rail sections are joined. The buck fence has crossed posts with rails riding the elbows and is sometimes called a Yankee fence, because a settler from the North was believed to have constructed the first one. In post-and-rail fences, the rails are stacked between double posts.

Variations of all four styles also can be seen. One variation of the post-and-rail type has wooden pegs inserted into holes drilled through the post to hold up the rails. In most post-and-rail fences, five or six rails are used in each section to get the fence high enough to hold stock. By using pegs, only three rails have to be used. Apparently the farmer who conceived this style figured that whittling pegs was easier than splitting rails. I had seen a long stretch of pegged fence back near Mile Post 159 the day before and had stopped to photograph it.

A section of picket fence also was displayed here. Mountain folks mostly used picket fences to keep varmints out of their gardens.

Less than a mile beyond the tower on Groundhog Mountain is the one-room log cabin where Aunt Orlena Puckett lived for 65 years until her death at 102 in 1939. Aunt Orlena was a midwife who delivered more than 1,000 mountain children, including a grand-grandnephew when she was 100. Ironically, she gave birth to 24 children of her own, none of whom lived past age two.

Two miles from Aunt Orlena's cabin, I caught a glimpse of Bluemont Presbyterian Church through the trees and stopped to get a photograph of it. This was one of six churches started in this area by the Rev. Bob Childress, whose life became the subject of a popular book, *The Man Who Moved A Mountain* by Richard C. Davids. Childress was a mountain boy who went away to college and seminary and returned home to bring mainline religion and education to his neighbors early in this century. The six churches he started were all built by the parishioners themselves from the white quartz so common in the area.

Learning why Orchard Gap was called that was easy. I only had to turn off the parkway and follow the signs down the mountainside to Levering Orchard, where it was cherry time, the most hectic time of the year for the Levering family.

People come long distances to be at Levering Orchard during cherry time.

"Let's see," said Virginia Price, a cousin of the orchard's owner, Sam Levering, as she checked a log of the hometowns of visitors who had arrived just within the past hour to pick their own cherries, "Winston-Salem, Toast, High Point, Pfafftown, Greensboro, Elkin, Westfield, Clemmons, Ararat, Asheboro, Mount Airy..." All of those across the state line in North Carolina.

FENCES 1: An example of a snake rail fence, made by piling rails on top of one another in a zig-zag pattern.

FENCES 2: An example of a post-and-rail fence, where the rails are stacked between double posts.

FENCES 3: An example of a buck rail fence, which has crossed posts with rails riding the elbows. It is sometimes called a Yankee fence, because a settler from the North was believed to have built the first one.

FENCES 4: An example of a pegged post-and-rail fence.

MIDWIFE'S HOME: The cabin of Aunt Orlena Puckett, a midwife who delivered more than 1,000 mountain children, including a grand-grandnephew when she was 100.

COUNTRY CHURCH: Bluemont Presbyterian Church is one of six churches started by the Rev. Bob Childress.

Nearby, Sam Levering's son Frank was guiding a group of visitors up the hill to the picking trees.

"We have a picture-perfect day," he was telling them. "We don't get too many days this pretty."

Frank grew up on the orchard but he was gone for many years, first to get a master's degree at Harvard, then to write screenplays in Hollywood for seven years. But he had returned to the mountains to tend the orchard and write books with his wife, Wanda Urbanska, whom he met in a writing class at Harvard, and who was now busy down the mountain at the packhouse, weighing cherries and taking money.

"Frank, I've never seen anything like this," one visitor said, pausing to grasp a tree branch heavily laden with dark sweet cherries.

"We don't know what we're going to do with them," Frank said.

Just up the hill in front of the big frame house that Frank's grandfather built, Sam Levering was waiting to greet visitors. A short, friendly man in his 80s, Sam was wearing Red Camel overalls and a big smile.

A Quaker, Sam helped to negotiate the United Nations Treaty of the Seas. He founded and led international peace organizations in which he was still active. He still travels widely making speeches for peace. But not in cherry time.

"That's a pink wax there," he told a visitor admiring a nearby tree. "They're not quite ready, but aren't they pretty?"

When Sam's daddy, Ralph, left Tennessee in 1907 to find the perfect spot for an orchard, he went about the hunt scientifically.

"He had walked 375 miles in and out of coves looking for a place in the thermal belt where frost doesn't come when he found this place," Sam told me.

The thermal belt is an area on the eastern side of the Blue Ridge Mountains, away from prevailing winds, where a band of warm air becomes entrapped between the cold valleys and the cold ridges above.

In every cove Sam's father asked farmers when the last spring freeze had killed the fruit crop. When he got to Alex McMillian's farm near Fancy Gap, Virginia, 12 miles north of Mount Airy, North Carolina, the answer was 1878. That was the best he found.

He bought the place and began setting out apple trees in 1908. His site selection proved wise. Only twice in the next 80 years – in 1921 and 1955 – would the orchard's crops be wiped out by frost.

Two weeks after Ralph moved his wife, Clara, and two young children into a log cabin on the farm, Sam was born.

Sam grew up working in the orchard and went away to Cornell University to study horticulture, particularly fruit raising. He taught for a while after college, then went to Washington during the Great Depression to help set up the Farm Credit Administration for President Franklin D. Roosevelt.

In 1939, he and his wife, Miriam, moved to the mountains to join his father and eventually to take over the business. The orchard expanded with the years, but it remained mostly apples until the '60s. Sam added peaches, plums, nectarines, apricots and finally cherries.

"At first we just planted a few trees around the house for home use," Sam said of the cherries. "They did splendidly and people came and wanted them. Finally, I decided that people really wanted cherries."

Now 25 acres of the 90-acre orchard are in cherry trees. There are 300 trees in full production, another 300 just beginning to come in and 600 young trees that will begin producing in a few years.

It's the only commercial cherry orchard south of the Potomac, Sam said, and one of the most diverse in the country, offering 23 varieties, 15 of dark, sweet cherries, five of wax sweets and four of tart pie cherries.

Unlike the other fruit, which is picked by professionals and shipped to many places including Saudi Arabia, Sweden, Iceland and the Dominican Republic ("If they've got the money and want the apples, well, there they go," said Sam), the cherries are all pick-your-own.

"My guess is we've had about six hundred people here today picking cherries," Sam told me, and it was only late morning.

He maintains a mailing list of 3,000 people, to keep them informed about when the different cherries and other fruits are coming in.

"They come back year after year because they like the cherries and there's nowhere else to get them."

Sam and Miriam reared six children at the orchard, and now have nine grandchildren. Two years earlier, Frank, their youngest son, had returned home to ensure that a third generation would keep the Levering Orchard going.

Not that Sam had any intentions of quitting.

"Father found a good place," he said. "One that we enjoy. And I enjoy the outdoor work. It obviously has not hurt my health. The Lord's been good to me. I can still head out, drive all day, speak and get up the next morning ready to go."

ORCHARD MAN: Sam Levering shows off a bucket of cherries. Visitors drive for hundreds of miles to pick cherries at Levering Orchard.

A little later, he stood in front of his house, watching a dozen visitors trooping down the mountainside lugging buckets brimming with fat cherries.

"What could a person want more than a wonderful family, a beautiful place to live and work that you enjoy?" he said. "I'm very fortunate."

Even before I'd reached Fancy Gap, I could hear the throbbing of the huge diesel engines of the big trucks passing on I-77, one of three interstate highways the parkway crosses. I stopped on the bridge for a moment, caught in the swirl of fumes, heat and currents stirred from below, to look at the traffic, before I pedaled back off into the beauty, tranquility and blessed relief of the parkway.

A few minutes later, I stopped to look down at the country's largest granite quarry near Mount Airy, North Carolina, a small whitish patch in the hazy distance. A big chunk of granite from the quarry was displayed at the overlook.

At the next overlook, a couple from Manchester, Tennessee, who were headed north, questioned me about my ride and told me that a big group of bikers was headed my way.

I rode on past more farm fields and pastures, by the ruins of a burned house with a mobile home parked beside it, past a dairy farm and a dead black snake and alongside a very pretty creek. For 11 more miles I rode, but I never did see that group of bikers and I couldn't help but wonder what had become of them.

Trip Progress Log, Day Seven: 30 miles
216 total miles completed, 253 to go.

DAY EIGHT

We had spent the night in Galax, eight miles off the parkway, a furniture-making town famous as a center for old-time mountain music. Each August since 1935, the finest mountain musicians have been drawn to Galax for the country's oldest and best-known fiddler's convention at Felts Park. It was only natural that when the National Park Service began thinking about building a center for mountain music along the parkway, Galax would become a natural choice for its site.

One of the biggest advocates of the music center had been Olen Gardner, a high school teacher, part-time preacher, mountain musician and judge of fiddlers' contests, who makes fine banjos of walnut, cherry and curly maple at his home in Riner in Montgomery County. I had spoken with him by telephone.

"You know, not so long ago you could go up and down this Blue Ridge crest and about every third house had music in it," he had told me. "That was the only entertainment that they had."

One house that had it for sure was the one in which Olen grew up at Fancy Gap, near the parkway, through which I had passed the day before.

"My people, they all played instruments," he said, "old homemade banjos and fiddles. I was playing a banjo when I was five years old."

Olen went on to become well known as a banjo player, especially for his old-time "clawhammer" style. For two years, he played at the famous Renfro Valley Barn Dance in Kentucky with Charlie Monroe, brother of Bill, who became known as the "father of bluegrass music."

"We use to call it hillbilly music," he said. "It never did get commercialized, so it never did have a good name."

Frequently, Olen dresses as an old mountaineer and plays his banjo

Text on headstone:

REBECCA SMITH MOXLEY
OCT. 20, 1890
JAN. 29, 1908
REBECCA DIED THREE DAYS AFTER
SHE GAVE BIRTH TO HER BABY SON
JOHNNY EDGER MOXLEY. HE WAS
RAISED BY HER PARENTS
JACOB AND SALLY SMITH.
JOHNNY MARRIED EMMA BRANNOCK
HIS CHILDHOOD SWEETHEART
THEY HAD THREE CHILDREN
ETHEL, ROSIE AND CORNELL.
STONE PURCHASED BY CHILDREN
ERECTED BY WHOLESALE MONUMENT
COMPANY —— MOUNT AIRY, N. C.

PARKWAY CEMETERY: Nineteen people are buried in this cemetery, the largest of several cemeteries on park land. The first person buried here was Rebecca Smith Moxley, who died three days after giving birth to her son in 1908.

at campfires and other events along the parkway. He loves the parkway as much as he loves old mountain music, and that's why he had been campaigning so hard to see that a center for mountain music got built on the parkway.

Such a center not only would preserve the distinctive mountain music but also would acquaint people with it who might never have heard it before, he said.

Olen told me he thought that the perfect spot for the center would be at Fisher's Peak, a conical mountain on the North Carolina line south of Galax. (Parkway officials later agreed with him, and acquired land for the center there, but as of mid-1993, construction funds still had not been budgeted by Congress).

"I just want to see it happen," Olen said.

Just a few minutes after starting my eighth day on the parkway, I was riding past the state line and the spot where the music center eventually will be. A half a mile farther on, I had reached Cumberland Knob, named for the English Duke of Cumberland, William Augustus, for whom the flower Sweet William also is named. Here construction on the parkway began. Here, too, was the parkway's first recreation area – picnic grounds, trails and restrooms built by youths from Civilian Conservation Corps camps during the Great Depression.

Near the restrooms is a cemetery, the largest of the several cemeteries on park land. Nineteen people are buried in it, including four infants. The first person to be buried here was Rebecca Smith Moxley, who at 16, pregnant with her first child in 1908, had a foreboding of death and asked a neighbor if she could be laid to rest at a favorite spot under an old apple tree on his land should something happen to her. Thinking that she was merely frightened of giving birth, the neighbor agreed. But Rebecca died three days after giving birth to her son, John Edgar, just three months after she had turned 17, and a small section of the neighbor's orchard became a cemetery.

Less than a mile from the recreation area, the Fox Hunter's Paradise Overlook offered a view of a knoll called High Piney Spur where local fox hunters use to gather to drink and tell tales while listening to their hounds running their prey.

After three and a half miles of short ups and downs, I descended to a stretch of the parkway that would be essentially level for the next seven miles, the first three miles of it following a beautiful trout stream called Big Pine Creek, the last mile passing through Roaring Gap, so

BRINEGAR CABIN: The cabin of Martin and Caroline Brinegar, built in 1880, is typical of a mountain homestead in the late 19th Century.

THE HOMESTEADERS: Martin and Caroline Brinegar. Each year, their descendants gather at the homestead for a family reunion.

named for its stiff winter winds. But the sweet ride ended at Little Glade Pond, another old gristmill site, at Mile Post 230. Over the next 10 miles I would be climbing more than 2,000 feet. The prospect was made a little brighter by the fact that even though the temperature was in the 80s, a strong and cooling breeze was blowing.

The view of Stone Mountain, a bare granite dome set in the foothills below, offered the first rest stop of the climb, two and a half miles and 400 feet in altitude later. Laurel blooming all around the parking area made the stop all the more refreshing.

Another steep incline led to a short but welcome downhill run to the Bullhead Mountain Overlook and the gap beyond. But then the climb became steep and winding once again. I took special note of the Mahogany Rock Overlook for several reasons. First, because it offered another break in the climb. Second, because it provided an interesting fin-shaped rock outcropping to examine. Once a big black, or sweet, birch tree – called mahogany by mountaineers – grew above this huge rock formation on the side of the parkway, thus providing its name. But the main reason I was pleased to be at Mahogany Rock was because it sits at Mile Post 235, marking the halfway point of my ride. From here on, the trip would be downhill, so to speak, even if all of the taller mountains along the parkway still awaited me.

The Devil's Garden Overlook, just half a mile downhill from Mahogany Rock, gave me a look into a deep, narrow, rocky gorge noted for its huge population of poisonous snakes, rattlers and copperheads. Some years earlier, an entrepreneur had erected a cable car across the gorge and tourists began flocking to it. Alarmed that an amusement park atmosphere would detract from the natural scenic beauty of the parkway, the Park Service bought the cable car, disassembled it and sold it as surplus to the city of Biloxi, Mississippi, which intended to use it to connect a close-by island park to the town's waterfront. Problems arose, however, and the cable car never got out of storage.

The view from Air Bellows Gap was of a fire watch tower on an adjoining mountain and of a farmer irrigating his fields with great sprays of water in the valley below.

A mile and a half of climbing later, I turned into the parking lot at Brinegar Cabin, a typical mountain homestead of the latter part of the last century, a spot I had visited many times before. Martin and Caroline Brinegar moved into this cabin as newlyweds in 1880, and made their way on the land for the next half century. The Brinegars were austere people who did not believe in music, dancing or drinking, and their photos etched into an exhibit near their home give them a dour appearance indeed. After Martin died in 1925, Caroline lived alone until the farm was acquired by the government more than a decade later. She lived nearby with a daughter until her death in 1943. She was buried alongside her husband on a sunny knoll not far from the cabin the two had shared. The Brinegars' homestead was preserved as it was, and each year, the huge Brinegar family gathers at the site for a reunion. On summer and fall weekends, rangers demonstrate mountain home skills at the cabin, which lies within Doughton Park.

Known as Muley Bob for his stubbornness and persistence, Robert Lee Doughton, was for many years a congressman in North Carolina's mountainous 9th District. As such, he fought to get the parkway through North Carolina – and his district. The park that now bears his name covers 6,000 acres of an area called the Bluffs. The park has trails, campgrounds, picnic areas, a lodge, restaurant, souvenir shop and gas station.

The restaurant at the Bluffs, where Linda and I had driven earlier for lunch, just two and a half miles from Brinegar Cabin, was my goal for the day, and I arrived with appetite aplenty for another meal.

Trip Progress Log, Day Eight: 25 miles
241 total miles completed, 228 to go.

DAY NINE

I got my earliest start of the trip on the ninth day, climbing onto my bike shortly after 8:00 a.m. at Doughton Park. Somebody was frying bacon in the nearby picnic grounds, and the aroma drifted out through the trees, awakening my hunger pangs. I intended to ride only about seven miles, mostly downhill, to Laurel Springs and meet Linda for breakfast before continuing the ride.

The ride began with a swooping downhill run along the face of a sheer granite cliff. Only a low stone wall separated me from a drop of several hundred feet, and as I swept down around it at high speed, I couldn't help but think how even the slightest mishap, say an animal running in front of my bike, could throw me right over the edge. I braked instinctively, but continued at a rapid pace.

Just as I was nearing the end of the run around the cliff's side, two yearling deer suddenly bounded from behind the stone wall alongside me. I was as startled as they, and none of us seemed to know what to do but continue in the direction in which we were headed: downhill. The deer raced along beside me for about 30 yards until we reached the end of the cliff and they saw an opening into the forest.

The morning was cool, and the downhill ride (not to mention the prospect of being tossed off a cliff) had chilled me. But at Alligator Back, a rock-outcropping that for some reason made early settlers think of a creature never seen in these parts, a climb began that quickly warmed me.

The view at Bluff Mountain Overlook of bluish green mountains rolling to the horizon was softened by the morning mist obscuring the distant valleys, a beautiful vision to help start the day. I had one more brief climb to the Basin Cove View before starting down through

PARKWAY CLIFF: Near Doughton Park, the parkway is cut into a sheer cliff.

PARKWAY FISHERMAN: After running many other types of businesses along the parkway, John Myers now operates a trout lake.

Meadow Fork Valley to Laurel Springs, where I had the biggest break-
fast of the trip: eggs over easy, bacon, sausage, gravy, biscuits and
plenty of hot coffee.

I needed a rest after that breakfast, and I stopped at a trout pond I
had spotted from the parkway to see if anybody was catching anything.

John Myers was sitting in the shade smiling while a young woman
named Melissa Poe excitedly reeled in a large fish. But before Melis-
sa's husband, David, could land the trout in a net, it leaped from the
hook and splashed back to safety.

"That would've been your first fish," Melissa told her 11-month-
old daughter, Sarah. "He jumped right off, that mean thing."

"Right now they're not bitin' like they did," John said. "Early
spring, late fall, that's when they bite best. When it's cool weather. Girl
caught one yesterday, though, weighed three and three-quarter pounds.
Biggest one's been caught this summer was five and three-quarter
pounds."

The parkway brings much of the business to John Myers' lake, but
that's nothing new to him. The parkway has brought him his livelihood
for more than half a century.

John and other members of his family had no objections when the
parkway took part of their family farm back in the '30s.

"We was for it," John said. "I knew it was going to bring money
into the community. We was back in the boondocks. There was no
power line through here, no telephones. There was nothing but a dirt
road."

As a young man, John got a job with the survey crew that was rout-
ing the parkway. Later, he took a construction job on the new road.

"Pick and shovel work, you might say. I was making 30 cents an
hour."

But John saw potential in all the other young men who had moved
into the boondocks to build the parkway.

"Every farmhouse around here was full of boarders. They'd take in
the workers on the parkway, you know, bed 'em down and give 'em
three meals a day for a dollar a day."

John realized that there was no place for the workers to gather and
relax. Neither was there a gas station nearby. So he constructed a small
building only a few hundred feet from the parkway's path, put a couple
of gas pumps in front and opened for business in the spring of 1935.

"It had a great big meadow in the back," John said, "and I put a ball field back there. I had a big ol' ironside icebox. I'd put three-hundred-pound blocks of ice in there and haul beer up from North Wilkesboro, and that'd make good drinkin' for them fellers, you know. That's where they'd spend their weekends, see. On a purty Sunday, I'd sell about thirty cases of beer out of there."

Business was so good that the next year John put up a two-story building across the road and opened a restaurant on the first floor and a dance hall on the second.

"It went good," he said. "Yeah, about two or three nights a week I'd have a square dance up there. It'd be crowded, yeah boy. Then as soon as they got the parkway opened up enough for people to travel on it, I opened me up a motel, Myers' Motel. The parkway just dumped the business in my lap, you might say."

Later, John opened another store and gas station, and his brother Bob opened a second motel. A little community grew.

"We used to have a lot of neon lights," John recalled. "People going by would see it lit up down there like a town, and they'd come down off the parkway and stop. We'd fill up every night."

The businesses John started are still there, but they're operated now by others. After 38 prosperous years, John sold out, bought himself a house in Daytona Beach and retired.

At first, he and his wife, Nora, stayed eight or nine months of the year in Florida and only came back to the brick house he'd built in the midst of his businesses in Laurel Springs for the summer. But as the years passed, he began spending less and less time in Florida and more and more back in the mountains.

Four years earlier, after 14 years of wintering in Florida, John had sold his house there and come back to Laurel Springs for good.

"They say you can take a boy out of the mountains but you can't take the mountains out of the boy," he said. "I just always enjoyed these mountains. It's a good place to be."

He owned 500 acres on a nearby mountainside, and there he built himself a cabin.

"Put me a lake across the front so I could sit on the front porch and fish," he said.

He let others fish in his lake until drought dried it up and killed his fish. That was when he decided to open a trout pond in another, bigger lake he owned down by the parkway. He'd built that lake 40 years earlier and stocked it with carp and catfish, but its banks had become overgrown and the lake had sat hidden and unused for years. He cleared the banks, raised the dam four feet, stocked the lake with trout and opened for business.

"I enjoy foolin' with fish and I enjoy people," he said. "Gives me something to do. I never liked being retired."

John and Melissa Poe, who live at Bunnlevel in eastern North Carolina, had caught four fish and were ready to go. This was the third day they'd come to the pond to fish for their supper. They were going to take the fish back to a campground just off the parkway and cook them later in the day.

"Put 'em in foil with butter and onions and set 'em in the fire," David said. "They're good, too."

John weighed the fish, put them in a plastic bag and rang up the bill at $2.50 a pound. He smiled as he watched David and Melissa get in their truck to leave.

"Y'all enjoy them fish now," he called.

I soon was on the parkway, headed south again, and after just over an hour of blue horizons and uneventful ups and downs, I turned into the parking lot of the Northwest Trading Post, where the crafts and wares of mountain folks from 10 North Carolina Counties are displayed and sold. Linda had been browsing there for some time, and I joined her. After that brief rest, and a soft drink break in the parking lot, surrounded by motorcyclists, I resumed my journey, Linda driving on ahead.

I was in Christmas tree country now, one of the biggest Christmas tree producing areas in the country, and tree farms were becoming a common sight. On I rode past Jumping Off Rocks, although I couldn't find out who or what jumped off them, and on to Horse Gap, where there were no horses but where Linda was waiting to take me to lunch. We drove into nearby Glendale Springs for country ham and fried chicken, and after lunch we stopped to see once again the beautiful and famous frescoes in a small country church there.

The wind was blowing stiffly when I returned to my ride, making my ascents more difficult and my descents slower. At the Lump Overlook, I took in the view of the town of North Wilkesboro, and read from an exhibit the familiar story of Tom Dula, pronounced Dooley, a Civil War veteran who once had been held in the Wilkesboro Jail and was later hanged for murdering his sweetheart. His foul deed made his name live on in a popular mountain ballad.

The next grand view, just two and a half miles away, was off the opposite side of the parkway, where Mt. Jefferson with its impressive 4,500-foot summit stood stolid guard over the dairy farms and Christmas tree farms surrounding the town of West Jefferson, home to North Carolina's only cheese factory and the country's only summertime Christmas celebration.

A small stream gushing from the mountainside created Betsy's Rock Falls a mile farther on, not much as waterfalls go but pretty nonetheless.

I had lost 400 feet in altitude in one mile before I reached Benge Gap and started up again. Just after leaving the Lewis Fork Overlook, I was distracted first by some wild flowers I had not seen before, tiny purple blossom clusters on high stems with long slim leaves, another one to look up in the flower book. My attention to the flowers was distracted by another sight I'd never seen before, an orange and black salamander that was actually hopping, frog-like, across the pavement. I became so engrossed in the salamander's erratic movements that I stopped and watched it disappear into the grass off the roadside.

A few minutes later, I pulled into the E.B. Jeffress Park, where Linda was waiting to take me into Boone, where we would have dinner and spend the night. But before we could leave, the alluring sound of the cascades of Falls Creek led us onto the nearby nature trail and into the deep forest to see the park's centerpiece, a sight beautiful enough to carry me until morning delivered me back to the parkway.

Trip Progress Log, Day Nine: 31 miles
272 total miles completed, 197 to go.

DAY TEN

Leaving the motel in Boone the following morning, my bike on the back of the car, I saw a dump truck turn a corner and strike a woman riding a bicycle, dragging both woman and bike underneath until the truck came to a halt. The woman, tangled in the mangled bike, was conscious but bleeding and hysterical. She could not be quieted by bystanders who, by the time I reached the scene, had crawled beneath the truck, trying to comfort her. A police car pulled up, lights flashing, and an officer went beneath the truck. I left when I heard the wailing siren of the approaching ambulance. A disturbing way to start a day of bike riding.

"Please be careful," Linda pleaded as I struck out from Jeffress Park. She returned to Boone, planning to meet me later for lunch at Blowing Rock.

It was another beautiful day, clear and warm, and try though I might to let the parkway's splendor and serenity put the awful sight of the morning behind me, I couldn't do it. I kept seeing the bike being swept beneath the truck and hearing the woman's cries on the wind. And I kept turning to look nervously over my shoulder at the sound of vehicles approaching from the rear.

I stopped for a look at a reconstructed mountain church, paused a little farther on beside a laurel thicket that had been overgrown by lush wild grape vines, the vines loaded with small green fruit. Clearly, it would be a good year for wild grapes, and for the birds and other creatures that feast on them. Not far away, a mama groundhog and her baby emerged from a weed patch for a quick look in my direction, and obviously not caring for my presence, retreated.

From the Elk Mountain Overlook, just beyond Mile Post 274, I could follow U.S. Highway 421 as it wound down the escarpment and stretched away through the foothills to North Wilkesboro. To the right, I could see Grandfather Mountain, my destination for the day.

From Deep Gap, the parkway more or less parallels U.S. 421 for a few miles, then swings south of the burgeoning town of Boone, home of Appalachian State University. Wild Cat Road passes beneath the parkway along this stretch, but there is no access from the parkway to this road for motor vehicles. That is no problem, of course, for a mountain bike.

I headed south down Wild Cat Road. The pavement ended a short distance beyond the parkway, and the road narrowed as it wound through thick woods down the mountainside. Another quarter of a mile and I came to the small frame house where Willard and Ora Lee Watson live, a house that Willard built.

The porch was alive with potted flowers, all abloom. Chickens scratched in the yard. And even though the day was hot, a wisp of smoke came from the chimney. Ora Lee still bakes her biscuits in a wood cook stove. Not even the approach of a stranger prompted Willard's old dog to stir from a nap by the front door.

Through the open door, I could hear Ora Lee's sewing machine humming in the front room. She interrupted her work to tell me that if I wanted to see Willard, I'd have to venture across the road to his dusty and cluttered woodworking shop.

Ora Lee and Willard are accustomed to strangers seeking them out. People do it all the time. Law, Ora Lee said later, neither of them could tell how many there had been over the years. Charles Kuralt had come once to tell America about Ora Lee's quilts, and lots of people had come after that, hoping to get one, though not many had been successful. Ora Lee, after all, is only one person, and she can sew only so much. People have a much better chance of getting one of Willard's toys.

"Cap'n, I've got toys all over the United States," Willard told me when I found him in his shop. "I got 'em in England, I've got 'em in France. I've got 'em in Germany. I've got a little covered wagon in a museum in Texas. People come here from everywhere. The furtherest away I reckon we ever had anybody in this shop was from Australia."

Hot though it was, Willard still was wearing a black corduroy coat over his overalls. And he hadn't bothered to take off his big black hat inside.

MOUNTAIN CRAFTERS: Willard and Ora Lee Watson stand on the front porch of their home on Wild Cat Road, near Boone.

"Took a cold," he said. "Pulled my longhandles off and it give me the awfulest cold you've ever seen."

He was working at putting a bridle on a wooden mule, a traditional mountain toy. Ol'-time mountain toys are Willard's specialty.

"I've made peckin' chickens, dancin' dolls, walkin' mules, baby doll cradles, sleds, carts, stagecoaches, covered wagons. I've made about everything. Slingshots. Lord, I've caused more little boys to get their tail-ends whupped than any man in the world."

A few of the toys Willard makes are for big boys. Risque was the word that came to mind when he brought out one.

"Right here's a little something ahead of anything you'll ever see," he said, demonstrating it proudly. "That's just as close as you'll get to Mother Nature. I've got a piece in the house, first piece I ever made. It's an ashtray with a nekkid woman on it. Carved it out of a piece of wood."

Willard, who's a first cousin of famed mountain musician Doc Watson, wasn't always a toy maker. He grew up with his grandparents just a mile away on Osborne Mountain and went off to find work at a lumber camp when he was 14.

"The bossman said, 'You're a little bitty thing and light too.' He said, 'What can you do?' That's just as plain as yesterday. I said, 'I'll take a-holt of anything you got.' He said, 'Come on then.'"

Willard was 19 when he married Ora Lee. "Me and her was tied together 63 years last October, and I still like her. She's the best biscuit maker I ever want to talk to. Now she can bake you a biscuit, Cap'n, that won't pull your snags out of your head."

They had six children, although one died in childhood, and they worked hard to rear them.

"I've cut timber," Willard said. "I've sawmilled. Walked down the creek here about two miles every day to a sawmill for two dollars a day. Pulled a cross cut saw. They ain't but one tool that's harder on a man's body than a cross cut saw and that's a jackhammer. I've coalmined. I've ditched." He even went off to Cleveland, Ohio, to work for a while in a battery plant.

"I've done near 'bout everything a man could do to feed children. Never been in jail. I was lucky about that. I've done things they could've put the key on me if they'd found out, but my grandpa told me, 'Son, anything that you can't stay ahead of, don't fool with it.' I tell you, though, young folks don't know what work is. I hate to say' that, but that's the truth. If they was to come a time like I seed it one time, I don't know. They'd be more stealin' and robbin'. Why, hit'd be pitiful."

Willard was in his 50s when he started making toys. For 25 years he demonstrated his skills at the State Fair in Raleigh, but he had given that up a couple of years earlier. Ora Lee always made quilts for her family, but after Willard started making toys, she began making a few quilts to sell. She hadn't been able to keep up with the demand since.

"I'm goina quit takin' any orders cause I'm gettin' too old," she told me a little later, after Willard had invited me over to the house to see some of her quilts, the ones that were just too pretty to sell.

This was the first year in memory that Ora Lee didn't have a big garden. "Just ain't able to tend it," she said. But she admitted that she still would be canning vegetables on her big wood stove later in the summer, as she always had done. The vegetables would be coming from the gardens of nearby children and grandchildren.

Willard, who's always raised his own hogs and cured his own meat, put in that he didn't even have a hog this year, although he acknowledged that he still might buy one before killing weather in the fall.

"I find that I've slowed down," he said. "You know, age will slow you down."

He had just turned 83, and Ora Lee was 80 now.

"People changes," he said. "Time don't change but people does. Time don't wait. No, hit don't wait a-tall."

After bidding farewell to the Watsons and returning to the parkway, I couldn't help but be struck by the contrasts between their humble house and the expensive chalets and palatial mansions that had been built on the mountainsides along the parkway by wealthy newcomers. Time surely was changing the mountains, and it seemed a sad certainty that the time soon would come when there no longer would be a place in the mountains for people such as Ora Lee and Willard.

At Mile Post 285, I stopped at Boone's Trace, where the Daughters of the American Revolution had erected a plaque honoring the pioneers who first opened these mountains for settlement, the ancestors of people such as Ora Lee and Willard. This particular spot was where Daniel Boone had crossed the mountains on his trek into the wilderness.

Somehow I felt that Daniel Boone wouldn't be pleased with what he saw if he could pass this way now, for not far away, near Aho Gap, was a fake condo castle with stucco turrets and brightly colored flags flying only a few feet off the parkway, hardly in keeping with the parkway's rural nature.

It made me want to hurry on through this part of my ride.

On my way downhill from the castle, I was startled to see a body lying in a gutter alongside the road. A clutch of fear caught my stomach. Had somebody been hit by a car? Surely I would not be seeing something like this twice in a single day. I braked to see what had happened, and a young man with long hair, a backpack and stereo earphones clamped to his head stirred from an apparent nap. He grinned almost guiltily, gave me a peace sign and on I rode, slapping at deer flies, which were numerous today and out for blood. I could hear the whistle from the old steam engine at Tweetsie Railroad, an amusement park between Boone and Blowing Rock.

Just past Raven Rock overlook, I caught my first glimpse of the huge high-rise condo that grotesquely straddles a nearby mountain top, a building that still makes the blood pressure rise in certain mountain friends of mine. Its construction caused such a stir that it eventually brought about a law prohibiting the erection of such buildings on North Carolina mountain tops.

Fancy summer homes and apartments became even more numerous as I neared Blowing Rock, one of the wealthiest resort towns in the mountains, and I was glad that I was nearing U.S. 321, where Linda would be meeting me, and that after lunch, I would be putting this section of the parkway behind me.

It was a two-mile uphill ride after lunch to reach Moses H. Cone Memorial Park. Wild flowers, wild strawberries, blackberries lined my way. At one spot I stopped and counted 13 different wild flowers in a single 10-foot-square patch, but I could identify only a few. Linda had told me what several of them were but I already had forgotten.

Moses Cone Memorial Park was named for a North Carolina textile magnate who was called the Denim King. At age 40, Cone began buying land near Blowing Rock and eventually acquired more than 3,500 acres. On it he built a self-sustaining estate that included a 20-room house that he called Flat Top Manor. The house became a summer home for Cone and his wife, Bertha.

Although Cone died in 1908 at 51, his wife continued to enjoy the house until her death in 1947. The estate was left to Moses Cone Hospital in Greensboro, North Carolina, which in 1950 donated it to the Park Service.

MANOR HOUSE: Flat Top Manor, the 20-room summer home built near the turn of the century by North Carolina textile magnate Moses Cone.

Now visitors may sit on the manor house's big front porch, taking in the view, walk or ride horses over the estate's 25 miles of carriage trails, or fish in the several trout ponds and bass lakes.

Linda was waiting for me at the grand house, and we toured it together, pausing at the shop operated by the Southern Highlands Handicraft Guild to watch a basket maker and a potter work.

The parkway wends for two and a half miles through Moses Cone Park, then passes into another park, Julian Price Memorial Park. Price was the president of Jefferson-Standard Life Insurance Co. in Greensboro. He acquired more than 4,000 acres near the Cone estate, and on it he built a 47-acre lake and several trout ponds and raised hogs and white-faced cattle. He often talked of moving to his mountain farm when he got old so that he could "really raise some stuff and have some fun." Unfortunately, he was killed in a car crash on his way to the farm in 1946.

His daughter, the late Kathleen Bryan, and Jefferson-Standard Life Insurance Co. donated the farm to the Park Service, and the park has become one of the most popular recreational areas along the parkway, offering fishing, canoeing, picnicking, camping, hiking and other activities.

I stopped at Sims Pond, which was stocked, a sign informed me, with native trout, creel limit five, size seven inches. The pond was ringed with trails and from one emerged a boy of 14 on a mountain bike. He stopped when he saw my bike and asked if I did any off-road riding.

"Only when I'm forced off by cars," I told him.

It was all he did, he said, and he really enjoyed it. But he quickly added that he rode only on existing trails.

"It's so pretty here," he said, "I don't want to mess anything up."

While we were talking, a luxurious new car with New York tags pulled up, and a middle-aged couple got out to admire the pond. When they returned to the car, a loud alarm went off. While the man fumbled frantically to shut it off, the woman started screaming at him.

"You idiot! You idiot!" she kept yelling.

"Nothing like a nice ride through the mountains to inspire peace and calm," I said to the boy, who laughed and rode off to one of his trails. I, too, left the screaming New Yorkers and their honking car behind.

I passed a big picnic area where a spirited volley ball game was underway and stopped a short distance later to admire the green, tree-lined waters of Price Lake. The sight of it made me wish I had brought along a fishing rod, even though the few people I saw fishing didn't seem to be catching anything.

Grandfather Mountain loomed just ahead of me now, and I soon passed onto the newest stretch of the parkway, the 7.2-mile section reaching around Grandfather's side that was for many years the parkway's "missing link."

It was miscalculation about the length of this segment that would cause the parkway's mile posts to be wrong for the remainder of its distance. The new segment had been 1.2 miles longer than planned, making the parkway's total distance 470.2 miles. The parkway's mile posts, in place for many years, measured the distance as 469 miles. Rather than change all the mile posts beyond this segment, the Park Service simply stretched out each mile along Grandfather Mountain to accommodate the extra 1.2 miles.

Climbing now, I stopped at Mile Post 300, just short of Green Mountain Creek to savor the moment. Only one more 100-mile marker to go. Graffiti marred the sign identifying Pilot Ridge Overlook. "I was hear," some genius had written.

At the Wilson Creek Valley Overlook, another magnificent view opened, and Grandfather now stood before me. I could see its famous swinging bridge near the peak, tiny figures walking tentatively across it. I was only a short downhill run from starting up Grandpa's boulder-strewn side, but that would wait until tomorrow.

Trip Progress Log, Day Ten: 30 miles
302 total miles completed, 167 to go.

VIADUCT TRAIL: This trail runs beneath the Linn Cove Viaduct.

DAY ELEVEN

Until September of 1987, the parkway simply ended when it reached Grandfather Mountain. Travelers had to take a treacherous 10-mile detour to rejoin it. Now a series of short, curving concrete bridges, railed with stone, delivers the road up the mountainside to a bridge that has become a major tourist attraction itself.

The Linn Cove Viaduct at Mile Post 304 passes just under the Black Rock Cliffs about 1,500 feet below Grandfather's peak, which at 5,938 feet makes it the highest in the Blue Ridge range. An S-shaped bridge that curves along the mountain's contours, it was built of 153 pre-cast segments, only one of them straight, at a cost of $10-million. It is said to be the most complicated segmental bridge ever built.

The long delay in completing the parkway, which wasn't finished until more than 50 years after it was begun, was caused by concern over preserving the environmental integrity of Grandfather Mountain. The viaduct was the solution.

Some travelers had described their rides across the viaduct as giving them the feeling of driving into space, and I had experienced that sensation myself. What I didn't know was how it would feel to ride a bike across it. But I soon would be finding out.

Big boulders had been spread alongside the parkway to prevent parking near the viaduct. Soon after the bridge opened, so many people wanted to walk onto it that a rule had to be imposed to stop it. Still people parked alongside the roadside to get out and take photographs. So "no parking" signs had to be erected. Not everybody obeyed the signs. Hence the big rocks. The Yonahlossee Overlook near the bridge's northern end had become one of the busiest along the parkway as visitors crowded in to hike back along the roadway railing to look at

BLUE RIDGE PATRIARCH: Grandfather Mountain looms over the parkway's newest segment, the Linn Cove Viaduct.

THE "S" BRIDGE: The top-down construction of the Linn Cove Viaduct solved the problem of how to preserve Grandfather Mountain while closing the gap in the Blue Ridge Parkway. (Photo by Figg and Muller Engineers)

the bridge and snap photos of it, and I joined them before climbing back onto my bike and riding across, with two other bike riders following.

The sense of riding into space was not there on a bicycle, perhaps because I was riding in the lane next to the mountainside, where I could look over into the rhododendron and boulder garden and see hikers on one of the trails that parallel the parkway.

Alas, the ride was over all too quickly, because the bridge is only 1,243 feet long, far shorter than it appears in some photographs.

Linda was waiting in the large parking area at the southern end of the viaduct, and we followed the trail under the bridge and onto the boulders above it to get a closer view and take more photographs. Soon, however, I had left behind rugged Grandfather Mountain and the graceful viaduct that helped to keep it that way.

At the Grandfather Mountain Overlook, a half mile past Grandmother Gap, I stopped to read a lengthy exhibit about salamanders. More species of salamanders live in the Southern Appalachians than in any other place on earth, I learned, and some mountains have their very own species, including Grandfather and Mount Mitchell, to which I was heading. But salamanders, tailed amphibians, are nocturnal and rarely seen except in mating season, I read. Now I understood why the salamander I had encountered miles back had been hopping. No doubt it was hopping with joy.

I soon had entered Pisgah National Forest, through which I would be riding for the next 48 miles, and at Mile Post 310, I arrived at the overlook at Lost Cove Cliffs, by far the parkway's most popular nighttime attraction. From this spot, on certain nights, can be seen the famous Brown Mountain Lights, a mysterious phenomenon that has never been satisfactorily explained, although it has been studied often. The star-like lights hang low in the sky, fading and brightening, disappearing and suddenly reappearing. Many explanations have been offered, but the mystery remains. The lights have even been the subject of a popular country song.

The ride was mostly downhill and easy to the Linville River, and I turned into the picnic area, where Linda was waiting to take me to a favorite little restaurant nearby. After lunch, we drove back to the 1.2-mile spur road that leads off the parkway to the campground and visitor center at Linville Falls. From the center, several trails lead to spectacular views of the falls. We hiked up to the cliffside view of the

LINVILLE FALLS: From the visitor center at Linville Falls, several trails lead to spectacular views of the Falls.

UPPER FALLS: Another trail from the visitor center at Linville Falls leads to Upper Falls.

Plunge Basin, then returned to the visitor center and took another trail to the Upper Falls. We didn't have time to take the longer hike to the view of Linville Gorge, a wilderness area long protected from loggers, where some of the largest hemlock trees on earth grow, but Linda and I had become lost there once when our son, Erik, now in his 20s, was only two, and we had had enough of the gorge and the hemlocks to last us a good while.

From the parkway's junction with U.S. 221, a mile from the Linville River, I would have a tough climb of nearly 700 feet up Humpback Mountain to Chestoa View. I was entering mining country now, an area of immense mineral wealth, and from the North Toe River overlook, a mile into my climb, I could see an open-pit kaolin mine in the valley to the west, near the town of Spruce Pine, and smaller mica mines on the far hillsides. While I was at the overlook, a Volkswagen passed on the parkway with three surf boards strapped to its top. Could the driver have taken a wrong turn somewhere?

Just past Mile Post 319, a view opened to the opposite side of the mountain, into North Cove. I stopped at a bridge across a small gorge to enjoy the view of Flat Top Mountain in the distance. To my right as I caught my breath, a massive rock was hanging over the parkway with laurel, wild flowers and a sassafras bush growing from it. The tooth-brush tree, my grandmother had called the sassafras, for she chewed its twigs and made them into teeth cleaners. If I could have reached the bush, I would have snapped a twig to chew out its fragrant flavor.

Chestoa View was worth the hard climb. From the parking area, where flame azaleas were abloom, you wouldn't know it was there, but a short walk led to a precipice that offered a view as dramatic as any on the parkway, one of those spots where I felt uneasy standing too close to the low rock wall that was the only barrier to the sheer drop below.

The ride down the other side of Humpback was almost as dramatic as the view at its top, momentarily giving me the sensation of free fall until I reached for the brakes and a safer descent.

I had caught glimpses of the railroad tracks looping down the mountainside even before I got to McKinney Gap. When I arrived, I could hear a train creaking, groaning and squealing as it started easing its way down.

I couldn't see it, for it was passing through a tunnel 400 feet beneath the parkway before it emerged into the trees to begin winding through a marvel of railroad engineering called the Loops.

Here the track originally laid for the Clinchfield, Carolina and Ohio Railroad, conqueror of the southern Appalachians, begins to break free of the mountains on its nearly 300-mile run from Elkhorn, Kentucky, to Spartanburg, South Carolina.

Nearly 30 miles of track had to be laid and 18 tunnels blasted and dug to cover the 12 air miles from the gap to the plateau 1,350 feet below.

I listened as the train made its way through the Loops. Then I turned off the parkway and rode a mile down a paved road into the community of Altapass, once a thriving railroad center, now a place where furniture is made. Down by the pallet shop, not far from the Baptist Church, a bright red Clinchfield caboose was parked on a tiny stretch of track, my destination. Inside was Lee Medford.

"Here's what Altapass looked like at one time," he said, showing off old photographs on the walls.

There was a depot, a switching yard, a maintenance shop, a big, green, company boarding house up on the hill where passing railroad men stayed, several company houses, a commissary.

RAILROAD MUSEUM: Lee Medford operates a railroad museum inside a bright red caboose at Altapass.

"Tore 'em all down," Lee said. "All the company homes and everything, they just tore 'em all down."

Lee's caboose is about the only reminder now of the railroad center Altapass used to be. He had bought it six years ago, put it alongside the little white house where he reared his family and fixed it up into his own little railroad museum.

Lee grew up near the Loops on the other side of the mountain in North Cove. As a teenager, he and his friends would gather at a spot where trains stopped to take on coal and water, hop onto one of the cars, ride to the gap and walk back home by Pepper's Creek.

Once, Lee got a special treat.

Fred Leonard, the legendary engineer of steam engine 558 on the CC&O, was known throughout the mountains as Foggison Bill because of the distinctive and mournful music he played on his steam whistle. Lee played harmonica as a teenager, and once he was playing by the tracks, imitating Foggison Bill, when the famed engineer stopped for coal and water, heard him and invited him to ride up the mountain in the engine with him.

On the ride, Lee talked Foggison Bill into letting him blow the whistle.

"He said, 'Go ahead.' I started trying to blow it and I was just making a mess of it. He said, 'Gimme that dern thing, you're goina ruin my reputation.'"

As a young man, Lee spent two years helping string a telephone line along the railroad track, then worked one winter on track maintenance before taking a job helping to clear land for the Blue Ridge Parkway. After working three years on the parkway, Lee opened a store in Altapass to compete with the railroad commissary. Next to it he set up a sawmill and began making crossties for the railroad.

Mountain railroading was treacherous, Lee knew, and in 1940 he went into the business that would occupy him for the next 40 years – salvaging the wrecks on the CC&O, which later became the Clinchfield, then the Seaboard, now the CTX.

At 77, Lee figures he's seen as many train wrecks as anybody alive, and pictures of many of them line the walls of his caboose.

"At one time, we had five on the ground at the same time," he recalled.

The biggest wreck he remembers happened 23 years earlier at Thermal City.

"They had a derailment of fifty-one carloads of coal dumped over a field, fifty tons to a car. I got as much out as I could. A whole lot of it's there yet."

Once at nearby Ashford, Lee and his men were just finishing cleaning up five carloads of coal by hand, when another train loaded with coal derailed at the same spot.

"We just had to run for the woods, you know. It was a pretty dangerous time, pretty exciting."

By the time Lee gave up salvaging wrecks a few years back, much had changed. Yet another company had taken over the line. All the old railroad buildings in Altapass were gone, as were Lee's store and sawmill. Many more trains passed down the line, but the tracks were improved and there were fewer wrecks.

Although retired, Lee said that he still couldn't bring himself to give up railroading. That was the reason for the caboose. He comes to it almost every day, he said, to listen to old train songs on an ancient hand-cranked Victrola, to pore through the railroad lore he's collected, or to reminisce with other railroad buffs who might happen by.

When he's not at the caboose, he might be found on the porch of his mountainside brick house near the parkway, listening to the trains creaking and groaning and blowing, always a comforting sound to him.

"But I miss those ol' steamers," he said. "I don't know how to explain it, but they were more or less like something alive. "Them whistles they had on them steamers, you ought to hear them ol' seven hundreds a-blowin'. Make the hair stand on your head."

Trip Progress Log, Day Eleven: 31 miles
333 total miles completed, 136 to go.

DAY TWELVE

Few places on earth can boast of having as wide a variety of rocks and minerals as North Carolina, which claims more than 300 varieties. Emeralds, rubies, sapphires, garnets, even diamonds can be found in the state, and North Carolina was the scene of the country's first big gold rush, the site of several early mints.

The area around the town of Spruce Pine is rich in minerals, and many are mined here, including mica, kaolin, tungsten, feldspar and quartz (the world's largest telescope at the Mount Palomar Observatory in California was made from quartz taken from a Spruce Pine mine). That explains why the Museum of North Carolina Minerals sits by the parkway at Mile Post 331 at Gillespie Gap, just five miles south of Spruce Pine.

I had visited the museum at least a dozen times before, but I always find it interesting, and I especially enjoy the brilliance of the fluorescent stones glowing in neon colors under black lights and the noisiness of the radioactive ores, so I began the twelfth day of my ride prowling once again through the museum, relearning all I had forgotten since the last visit.

I was facing a hard day, climbing more than 700 feet just over the first three miles, but I would be ascending more than half a mile before the day was over, reaching higher than I had yet been, so I was grateful for an opportunity to procrastinate.

Actually, although I was facing the second of the four great climbs along the parkway, I knew it was not as great as the first, and I was in better shape than I had been near the beginning of my ride, so I wasn't really concerned about it. Indeed, I covered the first three miles in less than 30 minutes, a personal record, I was sure, for so steep a ride.

ROCK SHOW: The Museum of North Carolina Minerals sits by the parkway at Gillespie Gap, near Spruce Pine.

At Little Switzerland, where we had spent the night at a lodge with a spectacular view, I encountered the second tunnel of my trip, the first in North Carolina. It was relatively short, only 547 feet long, and eerily quiet inside. Over the next 140 miles, I would be passing through 24 more tunnels, one of them nearly three times as long as this one.

This was a clear day but still hazy and hot, already in the 80s at mid-morning. I soon had reached my second tunnel of the day, much shorter even than the first, at Wildacres, site of a famous writer's colony started by a North Carolina Baptist-preacher-turned-writer, Thomas Dixon, whose most famous work was *The Clansman*, filmed as *Birth of a Nation*.

I paused at Deerlick Gap Overlook for sentimental reasons. Once Linda and I and a group of close friends had come almost every summer to nearby Burnsville to stay at the old Nu-Wray Inn and see our famous friend W.C. "Mutt" Burton appear at the Parkway Playhouse, after which we'd have a late-night penny-poker game. Those weekends always had been great fun, and they always had begun with a big picnic at this overlook. As I stood here now, reading an exhibit about groundhogs, I could hear the lingering laughter of dear friends at the empty picnic tables nearby.

Shortly after leaving the overlook, I caught my first glimpse of the majestic Black Mountains, highest in the East and my objective for the day. They were an impressive presence, even in the distance.

Laurel and flame azalea were blooming at the Crabtree Meadows Recreation Area at Mile Post 340, where a campground, picnic area, coffee and souvenir shop, gas station, amphitheater and hiking trails are to be found. Few visitors are aware that this area was built during World War II by conscientious objectors, many of them Quakers from Guilford, Randolph and Alamance Counties in the Piedmont of North Carolina, who spent the war years at nearby Buck Creek Civilian Service Camp, which was overseen by the former president of Guilford College in Greensboro, Dr. Raymond Binford, and his wife, Helen.

Less than three miles from Crabtree Meadows, the Black Mountains loomed directly ahead. Named for the spruce and fir trees that ring their peaks and upper slopes, giving them a dark cast, the Blacks may soon be in need of a new name, for the spruce and fir trees have been dying of unknown causes at an alarming rate. At the Black Mountain Overlook, the Park Service has erected a diagram identifying each of the peaks in the range. Towering over all is Mount Mitchell, at 6,684 feet the highest peak east of the Rockies. The parkway crosses Mount Mitchell just 1,000 feet below the peak, and I would be churning my long legs up its side later this day.

Back on my bike, as I was trying to put the tiny tape recorder on which I was preserving the details of my trip back into the utility bag on the handlebars, I dropped it and it bounced right over the ledge and disappeared down the mountainside. I panicked. Inside the recorder was a microcassette containing all my observations and voiced remembrances for the last 156 miles. I dropped my bike and went over the mountainside after it, scrambling among the rocks, briars and poison ivy, searching frantically, slipping and sliding and grabbing onto small shrubs to keep my hold on the earth, certain that at any minute I would hear the deadly whir of a rattlesnake. I searched for half an hour, going maybe 30 feet down, all to no avail. As I was pulling myself back up to the overlook in utter despair, there in a little clump of wild flowers, at eye level, was my tape recorder, intact, undamaged, just a few feet below the edge of the drop.

It was with great relief that I crawled back onto my bike and over the next mile lost more than 500 feet of the altitude I had fought to gain this day.

At Buck Creek Gap, I began the struggle to get it back, an effort made more discouraging by a road sign informing me that Mount Mitchell was still 16 miles away, Craggy Gardens 20. That was 20 miles, I knew, of almost constant climbing.

Less than a half mile from the gap, the Twin Tunnels presented themselves, one of them 240 feet long, the other 401, separated by only a few hundred feet. I waited, as usual, until no traffic was coming to ride through them. Water was dripping from the ceilings of both, and it was so cool inside that I almost was tempted to stay for a while.

Serious climbing began at Singecat Ridge, more than 1,200 feet over the next four miles, but the effort was rewarded with the spectacular views that began presenting themselves. Ahead, though, over the dark, brooding mountains, something more ominous had presented itself: black clouds.

Linda was waiting at Big Laurel Gap to take me to lunch, and unaware of nearby facilities, we had ended up driving miles to the little community of Celo, where we finally found hamburgers and ice cream cones at a tiny diner. On the way back to the parkway, we ran into a brief shower. By the time we reached the overlook where Linda had picked me up, dark clouds were all around and I could hear thunder in the distance.

I decided to keep riding, and Linda agreed to go from overlook to overlook ahead of me and wait in case I needed rescue from lightning or heavy rain.

Ferns and goatsbeard, a long-stem flower with a white blossom that resembles a fireworks spray (Linda had identified it for me) lined the parkway as I climbed toward my fifth tunnel of the day at Rough Ridge. At one spot, a laurel thicket was entwined with a vine unlike any I'd ever seen. The leaves were bigger than my head and resembled the leaves of the elephant ear plant.

Breathing hard, with the tunnel in sight, I stopped for a brief rest and sprawled in the grass with one foot across the other, enjoying the view with my hands behind my head. While I was lying there, a hummingbird flew up, hovered a moment not five inches above my foot, checking, I guessed, to see if I posed any threat. I held still and it dived over to suckle from a tiny red wild flower, a fire pink, right beside me. I told Linda about it when I got to the Licklog Ridge Overlook.

The view was obscured by clouds and distant rain, but it wasn't raining on the parkway yet and I decided to pedal on.

By the time I got to the view of Mount Mitchell, less than a mile farther on and more than 200 feet higher, the mountain had disappeared behind a bank of dark clouds. I paused to read the exhibit about Dr. Elisha Mitchell, a University of North Carolina professor, for whom the mountain is named. Dr. Mitchell died in a fall over a waterfall while trying to measure the mountain in 1857. He is buried on its peak.

Although it clearly was raining on Mount Mitchell, it wasn't raining on me yet, and I continued on, covering in short order the downhill mile and a half from the Green Knob Overlook to the third Deep Gap through which I had passed on the parkway. The thunder was closer now, but on I rode, climbing again, almost to the mile-high level, where, two miles beyond the gap, as the clouds above grew appropriately blacker, I crossed from the Blue Ridge range into the Black. From here on, every drop of rain that fell on the parkway would eventually flow into the Gulf of Mexico. Soon I could see a sheet of rain marching up the parkway not a mile away, and I swept quickly down to Black Mountain Gap, where Linda was waiting beside an ever-running natural water fountain to rescue me.

Trip Progress Log, Day Twelve: 24 miles
357 total miles completed, 112 to go.

DAY THIRTEEN

I was beginning this day's ride at the intersection of N.C. Highway 128, which led right to the top of Mount Mitchell, more than 1,500 feet above. But I had no intention of turning off here and indulging this diversion, especially not by bicycle.

I had been to the top of Mount Mitchell many times, and although the views from there were top-of-the-world wondrous – a genuine panorama unrivaled for thousands of miles – every time I had been there I had been cold, even in summer, and the wind was always blowing far harder than I thought necessary.

Not to mention that the last time I was there, while we were scouting the parkway only a few weeks earlier, my car's engine had vapor locked because of the altitude, and even before that had happened, I had become depressed because of all the dead trees at the summit. I did not want to risk having my engine vapor lock while I was trying to struggle to the top by bicycle. No, I would happily bypass the peak of Mount Mitchell on this trip.

I had gotten a late start, and it was nearly 11:00 before I left the parking area at Black Mountain Gap. Disorganized dark clouds still hung about, although there was no rain. Now and then the sun broke through, highlighting patches of mountainside like circus spotlights focusing on different acts, too many to watch at one time. A brisk wind cut through the gap as I departed.

I was still climbing around the side of Mount Mitchell, and although I was skirting its peak, I was riding past fir and spruce trees, which had caused the terrain to take on the appearance of a more northern climate. Maine, perhaps. Or Canada.

As I climbed, I had magnificent views off down the wooded slopes to the south, the sun and clouds creating mosaics of changing patterns, green and blue. Behind me I could see the stretch of the parkway over which I had ridden the day before.

The view soon changed and I saw a big blue eye in the green below, the reservoir for the city of Asheville, sparkling like a cat-eye marble under a spotlight ray of sunshine. Not far from it was a huge, reddish gash in the green, where somebody had been clearing a major tract of land. I turned from that ugly scar to beauty closer at hand: wild strawberries, just ripening.

The riding was surprisingly easy as I pedaled toward the highest spot on the parkway north of Asheville, second highest on its entire route, but before I got there, I crossed a narrow gorge that offered a chilling sight: a straight-off drop for a couple of thousand feet. Even a sky diver leaping from here would have plenty of time for free fall before opening his chute. I had no chute and hurried on to the second highest spot, marked by a helpful sign, altitude 5,676 feet.

A dip of 300 feet in altitude took me to Balsam Gap, and the ride down chilled me, but I was not through descending. I still had nearly 200 feet more to go to Cotton Tree Gap. At Balsam Gap, I had passed out of the Black Mountain range, through which I had ridden for only six miles. Now I was in the Great Craggies, and immense mountains that they were, they demanded some effort from me, a climb of 500 feet over the next three miles. By this point, I considered that hardly worth noting.

I stopped at the overlook for Glassmine Falls, where a wet-weather stream cascaded for hundreds of feet over the face of the mountain down which I just had passed, but the weather apparently had not been so wet in these parts lately, despite the rain of the day before. The stream was a mere trickle, barely discernible.

A view opened to the north now – a logging road, two patches that had been cut and reforested, the new trees still just youngsters – and for the first time in many miles I could see a few houses and tended fields.

As I pedaled upward, around a curve. Craggy Gardens appeared ahead, rounded peaks almost completely covered with Catawba rhododendron, all abloom, a rolling sea of green and lavender, one of the world's most spectacular natural gardens. For two weeks each June, when the rhododendron is blooming, there are few more beautiful spots on earth than this.

I had planned my trip along the parkway for early June for this very reason. I wanted to be here in the time of the rhododendron, the laurel, the flame azalea, and the bush honeysuckle, all producers of achingly beautiful blossoms, and all along the way I had been amply rewarded.

Rhododendron is the most common shrub along the parkway, its big, waxy green leaves providing color and an enveloping comfort throughout the year, its blossoming in late May and June bringing a beauty like no other. Three varieties of rhododendron grow along the parkway.

Dominant is rhododendron maximum, or rosebay rhododendron, also called great laurel, by far the largest of the three varieties. I had been seeing its fist-sized, pink-tinged-white blossom clusters all along my route. Rarest and smallest of the three is the Carolina rhododendron, which blossoms pink and often grows from rock outcroppings. I had recognized it in only a few places, most recently on Humpback Mountain. The Catawba rhododendron, with its purplish blooms, grows mostly at higher elevations, often in vast thickets.

Some visitors get confused when they talk to mountain people about rhododendron, because most local people call all varieties of rhododendron laurel. They call laurel, with its delicate, porcelain-like blossoms, ivy.

Rhododendron is heath, a low-growing evergreen shrub, and Craggy Gardens is a collection of three heath balds, mostly treeless areas covered with a variety of shrubs, spread over the top of Craggy Dome, Craggy Pinnacle and Craggy Knob, all more than 6,000 feet high.

From Graybeard Mountain Overlook, I could see the parking area at the gardens more than a mile away, and I could tell it was crowded. Linda was there, waiting for me, and I pedaled fast, eager to arrive.

Almost everybody at Craggy Gardens had a camera in hand, and it was hard to move without getting into the range of somebody's photograph. Indeed, somebody with a video camera had been taping me as I rode up the mountainside, and he continued as I crossed the parking area to the car, where Linda had been resting against a fender watching my progress. Flowers are never enough for a video camera. Action is demanded. If no buzzing bees or humming birds are about, even a skinny guy riding through the blossoms on a bike will do.

"Isn't this something?" I said.

"Beautiful," Linda agreed.

"I meant all the cameras," I said.

THE WINDING ROAD: The parkway snakes up into the Great Craggy Mountains.

While I was still straddling my bike, helmet in hand, looking down at the parkway winding just below the crests of the two mountains over which I just had passed, a big, olive-green military transport plane roared out of the clouds and dipped between the two peaks, no more than a couple of hundred feet above the parkway.

"Damn," said the man with the video camera, who had missed the shot while filming a fat woman trying to waddle up the trail to the top.

After I had gotten out my own camera, Linda and I hiked to the summit, savoring every blossom along the way. We lingered at the top, reluctant to let go of such awesome beauty. On our way back down, we were stopped by a man walking alone, who seemed about to burst to say something to somebody, anybody.

"This has got to be the most beautiful place that God ever created," he said, obviously relieved that he had put word to the feelings that were overwhelming him.

"It's even prettier at the top," I told him.

THE GREAT GARDEN: Catawba rhododendren in full bloom at Craggy Gardens, a heath bald atop the Great Craggy Mountains northeast of Asheville.

It was a half mile ride downhill through the Craggy Pinnacle Tunnel to the visitor center, which also doubles as a heath museum. Inside, I talked to seasonal ranger Rick Roberts, who told me that it was not a particularly good year for the rhododendron.

"I don't think Mother Nature knew what she wanted to do this year," he said. "Too dry. Too hot. Late frosts. I wouldn't be surprised to wake up tomorrow and find snow on the ground."

It would be mostly a downhill run from Craggy Gardens to Oteen, just outside Asheville, 18 miles away, with a dramatic drop of nearly half a mile, a swift ride surely. But as I was starting off, I heard the rumble of thunder beyond the distant ridges to the west.

After five quick miles, which took me through the Craggy Flats Tunnel, I had to pedal uphill for a short distance before starting down again. I was almost keeping pace with the other downhill traffic, but several cars had congregated behind me, and I pulled off at Mile Post 371 to allow them to pass.

Nearly four miles farther on, I stopped at the view of Bull Creek Valley and read the exhibit there: "The last buffalo seen in this locality was killed nearby in 1799 by Joseph Rice, an early settler."

"The very last damn buffalo," I said out loud, shaking my head. What a way to go down in history.

The valley below was criss-crossed with roads and crowded with houses, obviously without room for a lonely old buffalo.

The Tanbark Ridge Tunnel, the longest I had encountered so far, 746 feet, was just half a mile ahead, This tunnel would teach me a couple of lessons. Although I waited as usual to make sure that no cars were coming before I entered, the traffic was too heavy and the tunnel too long for me to be certain that I would make it through without encountering another vehicle. And that was exactly what happened. A car came up behind me while I was in the darkest section of the tunnel, and I wasn't sure that the driver would see me in time to slow enough to keep from hitting me. Fortunately, he did. But the experience frightened me, and I never wanted to go through it again.

This also was the first time I had been in total darkness inside a tunnel, and I had learned that the small light on my handlebars was inadequate. It cast a narrow glow, leaving a tiny spot of light on the pavement ahead of me, but I hadn't been able to see the tunnel's walls and I became disoriented because of it and almost lost my balance. If I had fallen or struck the wall, the car that had come up behind me would have run over me without question.

Even longer tunnels lay ahead, and I knew I would have to take other measures when I got to them.

I told Linda about this when I met her at Bull Gap, just beyond the tunnel, to go to lunch in Asheville, and she offered the obvious solution. From now on, she would wait for me at tunnel entrances and follow me through, protecting me from traffic and lighting my way, as she had been doing in so many other ways for so many years.

We drove to a Mexican restaurant in Asheville, where I had a spicy lunch of chiles rellenos. While we were eating, a fierce storm struck. It showed no signs of abating soon, so we went ahead and got a room at a nearby motel to wait it out. I wanted to make at least 15 more miles today, but the storm had stalled over the Craggies. From the window of our room, I could see the lightning flashing repeatedly over the peaks. The storm raged for more than four and a half hours while I paced back and forth to the window, looking at the angry sky. By the time the recalcitrant storm had spent its energy and moved on, it was too late to resume my ride. I'd made only 19.9 miles this day, the shortest run so far.

Trip Progress Log, Day Thirteen: 20 miles
377 total miles completed, 92 to go.

DAY FOURTEEN

I was up at daybreak, eager to get going. I didn't want to wait for breakfast. I would finish my ride down the mountain, I told Linda, and meet her at the Folk Art Center near Oteen. We could go to breakfast, then she could check out of the room while I continued on around Asheville. The day promised to be uneventful, for there was little along this stretch of the parkway. Mainly, I would be making distance, connecting to more interesting spots beyond.

By the time we had reached the parkway and started up, we were enveloped in a fog so dense that it was hard to see the turns in the road ahead.

"Should you be trying to ride in this?" Linda asked.

I knew that I shouldn't. It would be particularly dangerous coming downhill at speed, but I thought that I could see well enough to make the turns. And this early in the day there would be little traffic to be concerned about. Moreover, I was familiar with this stretch of roadway. I had taken a test ride over it a few weeks earlier.

"Maybe it'll clear up," I said.

Within three miles, we had run out of the fog and right into morning sky. The sun was just beginning to peek over the Craggies, turning the billowing fog that hid the valleys into a golden shroud, a scene that caused us to stop in awe. It lasted only a few minutes, the wealth of gold trickling away with the rising sun. It had been a fluid beauty, unconcerned whether it was seen or not, but we had been in just the right spot at just the right moment to catch and hold it ever so briefly. I felt undeserving of such a gift and overwhelmed that I had been given it, even though it had been so quickly taken back. I had thought that this was going to be an uneventful day and already we had experienced

120

an event of soul-touching magnitude. The parkway, I had been told, was never without surprises, and this was just confirmation of that truth.

After I had reached my starting point and set out, I kept stopping on the way down to admire the fog below. All the mountain tops had been turned into islands in this sea of gray and white. Quickly, silently, that sea reached up and pulled me in. I sank faster and faster into its chilly dampness, and I was glad to see the Folk Art Center appearing through the mist.

I warmed myself drinking hot coffee and eating corned beef hash with poached eggs and home style potatoes at a restaurant off the parkway. While Linda worked the crossword puzzle in the morning newspaper, I read about my destination for the day: Mount Pisgah.

Pisgah was, of course, the name of the mountain from which Moses first viewed the Promised Land after leading his people out of Egypt.

Nobody knows for certain who gave that name to an imposing mountain that rises from the French Broad River southwest of Asheville, but there is little doubt why. The lush and fertile valley of the French Broad made many early settlers think of the Promised Land.

So impressive was this river valley that George Washington Vanderbilt, grandson of shipping magnate Cornelius Vanderbilt, began buying thousands of acres of it late in the last century. For good measure, he also bought Mount Pisgah, all 5,749 feet of it. From his mountain top, he could look down on all of his holdings, which included more than 130,000 acres of land and his humble home, a 250-room French chateau called Biltmore that was completed in 1895. Vanderbilt's descendants still live at Biltmore, which with its period furniture, great works of art, vast gardens and commercial winery is now operated as a major tourist attraction. Mount Pisgah, like most of the rest of Vanderbilt's land, is now part of Pisgah National Forest.

The Folk Art Center had not been open when we were there earlier, but it was now, and we went in to see the museum and browse in the gift shop, where works of members of the Southern Highlands Handicraft Guild are sold. Guild members regularly demonstrate their crafts at the center. And programs about mountain culture are presented often in the center's auditorium: music, dancing, lectures, story telling, and the annual Gee-Haw Whimmy Diddle contest.

Upstairs near the museum is a research library. I wandered in and met Rosemary Maxwell, who was for 25 years an Air Force librarian before she retired to Asheville and volunteered to establish the crafts library in 1982. She had accumulated several thousand volumes about crafts as well as many periodicals, records of the guild and individual histories of many of its members, past and present.

The library is open to all, Rosemary told me, although books may be checked out only by guild members. Students from all over come to research at the library, she said, and many others call to ask questions about mountain crafts.

"If we've got it," she said, "we'll find it."

As I was leaving the center, walking down the steps to the sidewalk, a dollar bill came rolling toward me on the wind. Nobody else was in sight, so apparently it hadn't just been dropped. Obviously, this was a day for unexpected gifts. I snatched up the bill, took it inside and left it in the contributions box.

I wasn't looking forward to the next 12 miles or so. I knew that I was coming to the busiest section of the parkway. More tourists got on the parkway here than anywhere else, but the parkway around Asheville also served as a shortcut and commuter path for local people, just as it did at Roanoke, and they always seemed to be in a hurry.

I quickly crossed U.S. Highway 70, the Swannanoa River and Interstate 40. As I was climbing toward Mile Post 385, a car came to a stop in the opposite lane and the driver waved me down.

A man and a woman were inside, obviously husband and wife.

"Can you tell me where the Blue Ridge Parkway is?" the man asked.

"You're on it," I said.

"You mean there ain't no park," the woman said.

"Well, it's a park for 470 miles," I said. "The road is a park."

"Oh, I thought there'd be a park," the woman said.

"There's a visitor center right up the road here," I told them. "You should stop in there. They can tell you all about it."

They drove away looking disappointed and bewildered. Heaven only knows what they had expected. A Mountaineerland amusement park?

On I climbed in unending traffic, the most I'd seen on the entire trip, almost all of them speeding. Some cars seemed to be going at interstate-highway speeds. It made me watchful – and nervous.

At the intersection of U.S. 25, the parkway began passing through the grounds of Biltmore Estate, the entrance to which was just three and a half miles north, but the grand house itself, which has been called America's finest castle, was not in sight.

The bridge across Interstate 26 made me as nervous as the fast, heavy traffic. Nicknamed "Mile High Bridge," it seemed as high as the bridge over the Roanoke River, and like that bridge, it was a magnet for those bent on suicide. I waited until no traffic was coming before I ventured onto it, staying well away from the railing and trying not to look over the side, pedaling hard through this man-made gorge where strong winds blew.

The ride was easy to the French Broad River, which had been muddied from the previous day's rains. I paused on the high bridge to watch a group of canoeists paddling downstream, each canoe a spot of bright color on the brown river: red, green, blue and yellow.

Just beyond the bridge, I stopped at the overlook to read how the river got its name. The story was not as racy as the name implies: "Prior to 1763, when the land drained by this river was claimed by the French, hunters and traders called this the Broad River for its wide adjacent lowlands. They soon discovered, however, that there was another Broad River in English territory just east of the Blue Ridge. So they started referring to this one as the French Broad River."

Here began the third great test for a bicyclist riding south on the parkway, a climb of 3,000 feet over the next 14 miles. And it was going to be another 90-degree afternoon. Before attempting it, I decided to take a break to visit the nearby Asheville Farmer's Market, probably the best farmer's market in the state, and fortify myself with lunch.

A mile after I had started my climb at mid-afternoon, I was stripped to shorts, dripping with sweat and regularly hitting my Gatorade bottle. The situation was almost identical to my climb up Apple Orchard Mountain. Views of the river valley soon opened, and they were something less than rustic: a big factory below, a power plant on a distant lake. On I struggled, sweating and breathing hard, working my way back to wilderness.

Linda was waiting to lead me through Grassy Knob Tunnel, 600 feet long, and the refrigerator coolness of its interior was a welcome respite indeed. Only two miles ahead was the longest tunnel on the parkway, the Pine Mountain Tunnel, 1,320 feet of dark, damp coolness. About two-thirds of the way into the darkness, I heard a car coming fast from behind, then a horn blowing loud and unendingly, the sound

RIVER BRIDGE: This parkway bridge spans the French Broad River.

CANOEING COUNTRY: Canoeists are drawn to the French Broad River and other streams along the parkway.

bouncing off the walls of the tunnel and echoing through my brain. I pulled over as soon as I emerged and Linda stopped behind. The other car raced on around, horn still blowing.

Linda looked frightened.

"What was going on in there?" I asked.

"If you'd been in there by yourself, you'd be dead," she said. "As fast as he was going, there was no way he could have seen you in time and slowed down enough to keep from hitting you. He almost hit me."

From the Bad Fork Valley Overlook, I could see the TV tower on top of Pisgah, and it looked a discouragingly long way up and away.

The triple tunnels of Ferrin Knob lay just ahead, all of the short, the longest only 360 feet, and we made it through them without incident.

The Stony Bald Overlook presented a nice view but nothing stony or bald, causing me to wonder why it was called that.

As I approached the Young Pisgah Ridge Tunnel, a female park ranger was busy changing a flat tire for an elderly woman. She looked up from her work to wave as I passed. Still another tunnel lay another mile ahead, the Fork Mountain Tunnel. Blackberries were hanging over the tunnel entrance, and watercress was growing there. It was my last tunnel of the day. Just beyond, at the view of Hominy Valley, we stopped, loaded the bike onto the back of the car and rode the rest of the way to the mountain top with ease.

Trip Progress Log, Day Fourteen: 29 miles
406 total miles completed, 63 to go.

DAY FIFTEEN

A storm had come with morning, making me get a late start on the rest of my climb to the top of Mount Pisgah. I had only four and a half miles to go, rising about 900 feet, and it might not have been so difficult if the temperature hadn't already climbed to 90 by the time I got back to the view of Hominy Valley to start my ride. Two more tunnels lay ahead, and traffic was heavy, so Linda drove on to the first tunnel to wait for me.

My whole body soon was running with sweat, and the coolness of the tunnels, only a few hundred yards apart, was welcome.

Linda drove on the Mount Pisgah Inn, leaving me to make the last mile and a half to the top on my own.

We had spent the night at the rustic inn and had dinner in its dining room, with its huge windows and breath-taking views of Vanderbilt's former domain. The dining room is famous for its rainbow trout prepared five different ways (six is you count the smoked appetizer) and filleted at table. I'd had my trout French style, in honor of the Vanderbilts, broiled and topped with a cream sauce dotted with baby shrimp. After dinner, a friendly college student waiter had asked if we would like to try one of the fruit cobblers.

"They're homemade," he said. "Aunt Bea made them just today."

"Aunt Bea?" I said.

That was what everybody called this wonderful woman who had been at the inn forever, he explained. She was famous for her cobblers and pancakes.

How could we resist? We shared a bowl of blackberry cobbler and it was delicious.

This morning, I had been fueled up the mountain by Aunt Bea's pancakes. At breakfast I had asked to meet her, but she had been too busy in the kitchen to take time to talk. She could see me later if I planned to be around, she had said, and I had arranged for her to meet us at lunch.

Her name was Beatrice Anderson, I learned, after she had joined us in the dining room. She was 76 and her home was in New Hampshire. But for the past 23 years she had lived from June to November on top of Mount Pisgah, staying in a dorm (actually the original inn) next door to the dining room with the college students who make up the bulk of the inn's employees.

She had gone to work as a waitress when she was 15, she said, had been working ever since and had no plans of quitting any time soon.

"I think if you keep busy, you know, you more or less have a good outlook on life," she said.

Bea was working as a waitress at a hotel in Palm Beach, Florida, when the hotel's owner took over management of Pisgah Inn and asked her to come to work in the mountains. She worked in the dining room as a waitress for 15 years ("Oh, I filleted so many trout!" she said) before she moved over to the kitchen. For 13 years, she continued to work in Florida every winter and the inn every summer. She had given up working in Florida 10 years earlier, but she couldn't give up Mount Pisgah.

"I love it here," she said. "It's so beautiful, and everybody's so good to me. I like my work. I really enjoy it here. It's my second home."

It was a downhill run to the view of the Pink Beds, a five-mile stretch of laurel and rhododendron in the valley below, but no pink blossoms were to be seen from this distance, indeed no color other than blended green. Beside me at the overlook, though, were brilliant yellows and oranges of flame azaleas.

Somebody had tried to rip the Cradle of Forestry exhibit from its stone foundation at Mile Post 411, but had failed, so I was able to read how George Vanderbilt had hired a German forester named Carl Schenck to manage his vast woodlands. Schenck had started a school on the estate to train foresters to assist him, the first school of forestry in this country. Vanderbilt's woodlands later became the nucleus for this country's first national forest. The buildings of the forest school have been restored and are open to the public, just off U.S. Highway 276 in the valley below.

STONE AERIE: Looking Glass Rock, where peregrine falcons nest.

A COOL SWIM: The falls at Graveyard Fields is a popular swimming hole for local people on the parkway.

From the Pounding Mill Overlook, I could look back at Pisgah and see the rangers' houses on the top and the route I had followed down.

A series of stone-faced mountains presented themselves at Log Hollow. One was Looking Glass Rock, a huge mound of granite with a rounded, sheer 400-foot cliff facing the parkway. I got a closer look at it from the overlook at Mile Post 417. This was the place the last peregrine falcons in North Carolina had nested before they became extinct in the state in the 1950s because of pesticide use. In 1984, however, the Wildlife Services of the United States and North Carolina had begun a program to reintroduce the peregrines, and this was one of the first places where they had been released. A pair was nesting on the rock, I had been told, and I remained at the overlook for a while searching the sky for a glimpse of them, but the wait was as futile as the peregrines' nesting turned out to be, for later, I would learn from a park ranger that the pair had produced no eggs.

Linda was waiting for me at Graveyard Fields, less than two miles from Looking Glass Rock. Some of the college students at the inn had told us not to miss this spot. It was the favorite local swimming hole, and the number of cars at the parking area confirmed its popularity.

Many years ago, a big wind had blown over many trees in the rocky hollow below the parking area, where the East Fork of the Little Pigeon River flowed. With time, the trunks of the dead trees had weathered until they had come to resemble a huge field of tombstones, and people had started calling the hollow the Graveyard Fields. The name remained even after a big fire destroyed the old tree trunks in 1925. Several trails led from the parking area to a series of falls along the river, one of them three miles away. We hiked through the heath down Rocky Bluff to Yellowstone Falls where several dozen people were sunning on the rocks and swimming in a huge stone bowl at the base of the falls. We sprawled on the rocks ourselves until the sun began to disappear behind gathering clouds and I heard a distant rumble of thunder.

We barely made it back to the car before the storm hit, wiping out riding for the rest of the day. Storms had made this day's ride the shortest of all: only 15 miles.

Trip Progress Log, Day Fifteen: 15 miles
421 total miles completed, 48 to go.

DAY SIXTEEN

I had originally thought that 16 days would be all that I would need to complete my ride, but now the sixteenth day was at hand and I still had nearly 50 miles to go, including one of the most difficult climbs on the parkway. I would need at least two more days – and maybe more than that, for I had awakened to find heavy fog clinging to the tops of the high mountains where I would be riding this day.

I had thought the fog might depart as the sun rose higher, but that had not been the case, and at mid-morning I had decided to ride in it.

Leaving Graveyard Fields, I climbed 200 feet in a quarter of a mile to the View of John Rock, where no rock was to be seen, indeed no view of any kind except for fog, and on I climbed.

At the road to Shining Rock Wilderness, the fog thinned enough for sunshine to begin filtering through it, and I allowed myself to hope that I might be escaping it. No such luck. The fog quickly mustered its strength and grabbed me again. It even followed me into the Devil's Courthouse Tunnel.

The Devil's Courthouse is a rugged rock face near Mile Post 422 that conceals a cave where the devil, according to legend, is supposed to hold court. Cherokee Indians believed that at this spot their Great Spirit sat in judgment of those lacking in courage. The courthouse attracts many who are not lacking in courage, and they often can be seen dangling from ropes on the cliff, which is one of the most popular spots along the parkway for rock climbers.

The only climbers to be seen this day were at the edge of the parking lot near the trail leading up the fog-shrouded rock, seven boys ages nine to 13 and two adults, all from Camp Chosatonga at nearby Balsam Grove.

"I'm afraid of heights, too," Steve Longenecker, a public school teacher from Asheville, was telling the boys when I rode up. "That's why I use all this safety equipment."

Steve, I soon learned, was the climbing instructor for Camp Chosatonga, and he and Peter Brezny, a camp counselor, were leading the boys through a practice session, fitting themselves in harnesses and linking themselves together with ropes and hooks before heading up onto the rock. This would be the second climb for the boys, and some of them seemed a little anxious about it. Their first climb had not been nearly so intimidating as this one.

"You're afraid of heights?" one of the boys said to Steve, his voice betraying his disbelief.

"Oh, yeah, you'd be stupid not to be," Steve said.

"It's really very safe," Peter told me as I watched the boys, some of whom seemed bored by all this practice. "Everyone is on a rope, and the only one in any danger would be Steve, who is the lead climber."

"People think this rock climbing is so dangerous," Steve said. "I think there's a lot less danger here than in riding horses or canoeing because those things are unpredictable. This is so predictable."

Making it predictable was the reason for all the practice, and I watched until the boys had made it through all the steps.

"Okay," Steve told them, "you did very well for a simulation. Now we'll see how you do when we get on the actual rock."

I had climbing of my own to do, so I wished the boys good luck and rode on into the fog.

Up to this point, the parkway had been following a southerly route, but just beyond the Devil's Courthouse it turned west. I wouldn't have known it if I hadn't had a map, for the fog deprived me of any sense of direction. It also kept me from seeing Herrin Knob, Wolf Mountain and even Rough Butt Bald, where Linda was waiting to take me to lunch.

When I returned to continue my ride after lunch, however, the fog finally had lifted, and I began a four-mile climb to the highest point on the parkway – 6,053 feet – on Richland Balsam Mountain.

I was in bear country now, and my next three stops were testament to it: Bear Pen Gap, Bear Trap Gap, Bear Trail Ridge. I'd never seen a bear on the parkway, but an exhibit at Bear Trap Gap had warned against feeding them. "Beggar bears are often rude," the exhibit had informed me in the only burst of verse I had encountered along the parkway. "They eat fingers as well as food."

Three-quarters of a mile from the top of Richland Balsam Mountain, I stopped to gaze out at the Cowee Mountains, from which great fortunes in rubies, sapphires, garnets and other precious stones have been dug, where, no doubt, even at this moment some people were finding gems in buckets of rock and dirt at the many tourist mines near the town of Franklin.

Many people stop to have their photographs made by the big sign proclaiming Richland Balsam Mountain to be the highest point on the parkway, and I was no exception. I had to wait my turn for Linda to snap my picture posing with my bike. The peak of the mountain, 357 feet higher, was covered with the bleached bare trunks of dead fir and spruce trees, resembling giant bones protruding from the mountain top, a depressing sight that I was not reluctant to leave behind.

It would be mostly downhill for the next 12 miles to my stopping point for the day, the town of Balsam, nearly 3,000 feet below.

The Roy Taylor Forest is a 31,000-acre tract within the Nantahala National Forest named for a local congressman who was a champion of the environment. At an exhibit honoring Taylor, a wooden deck protrudes into the treetops. Signs along the walkway explain the forest eco-system. It is a place of great beauty and tranquility, but every sign along the way, as well as the deck itself, had been covered by graffiti.

"It is graced and so untouched," somebody had felt moved to scrawl.

"At least until this idiot touched and disgraced it," I noted to my tape recorder.

Near the Steestache Bald Overlook grew one of the biggest American chestnut trees known, 17 feet in diameter and more than 100 feet tall, and an exhibit at the overlook honors the long-gone chestnuts, killed by an imported blight.

The descent was steep as I passed through Pinnacle Ridge Tunnel and stopped for great views of the community of Saunooke and the town of Waynesville before sweeping on down the mountain at a speed greater, I'm sure, than the limit allowed, to Balsam Gap and the town of Balsam.

Balsam is sometimes called the town that time forgot. Once it was a thriving center of commerce with two logging companies, five stores, five churches, a bowling alley, two schools, a restaurant, the railroad depot, the post office, a gazebo called the Roundhouse, where dances were held, mineral baths and, of course, the hotel.

HIGHEST POINT: The peak of Richard Balsam Mountain, the highest point on the parkway, is covered with the bleached bare trunks of dead fir and spruce trees.

Things are much different now. The logging companies moved out long ago after all the timber was cut. The last store, Knight's General Store down by the railroad tracks, closed a few years back after Billy Knight had a stroke. The bowling alley, restaurant, mineral baths and the Roundhouse remain only in aging memories. The last school is now a community center.

The depot was moved up the mountain some years ago to become part of a bed and breakfast place. Two trains still pass through town every day, freights on their way from Canton to Murphy. The post office remains, too, along with one church – Baptist – and, of course, the hotel.

When it opened in 1908, the Balsam Mountain Inn was the epitome of elegance. "The Hotel of the South," it was called. Guests arrived by train from the sweltering lowlands throughout the South, many of them bringing steamer trunks to spend the whole summer in mountain coolness.

The hotel was a sprawling place perched on a mountainside, a huge frame building painted white, three stories tall, with 100 guest rooms and a white-columned two-story veranda reaching for 100 feet across the front where guests gathered to chat, to enjoy the mountain view and watch the trains go by.

Guests still gather on the veranda for those purposes.

"That's the big excitement, sitting out there waiting for the train twice a day," Sarah LaBrandt told me with a laugh.

To step into Balsam Mountain Inn is to step back 80 years. Little has changed except that which time has wrought. Guests sleep in old iron beds with gallant but sagging springs. They bathe in claw-footed tubs. Ancient wicker fills the lobby, and the desk and its attendant equipment were there when the hotel opened, as was the huge and ornate walnut buffet in the dining room. The third floor is left now to ghosts.

Air conditioning? The hotel never had it. TV? Well, there is one, in the old reading room off the lobby, the room with walls covered with paintings of the hotel done by guests, but it gets only one channel and only a few guests seriously addicted to soap operas ever watch it.

"Our rooms are not deluxe," Sarah said. "They're clean and simple. It's not the Holiday Inn."

Then again, the rates aren't quite the same that other, more modern hotels charge, and they include breakfast and dinner. Lunch? Well,

MOUNTAIN INN: A view of the Balsam Mountain Inn.

A ROCKING PORCH: Guests at the Balsam Mountain Inn gather twice a day on the veranda to watch the train pass below.

there's the self-service honor-system "Country Kitchen," a small antique-filled room off the dining room where homemade soup is a dollar a bowl and coffee is always a nickel a cup.

The food is the province of Sarah's husband, Bob, who's been cooking at the inn each summer for more than 20 years.

"That's what brings the people back," said Sarah. "You don't go away hungry. His cooking really brings our people."

Fresh vegetables are Bob's specialty. Until 10 years ago, the hotel had a gardener and a huge garden from which all of the vegetables came for the dining room, but now Bob must go shopping for them each day.

Sarah and Bob lease the hotel. They took over its operation from Bob's parents, Don and Elizabeth LaBrandt, who ran it for nearly two decades.

Elizabeth started working at the hotel as a summer hostess in the '50s, and she and her husband took it over when the previous operators fell into ill health. Bob and Sarah, who now work winters at the greyhound track in St. Petersburg, Florida, where they live, started working summers at the hotel with their three young daughters in 1968.

"They were brought up all waiting on tables," Sarah said of her daughters, who still help out each summer.

The sense of family at the hotel extends to guests, many of whom have been coming every summer for decades. When Bob's parents ran the hotel, no children were allowed and the guests were almost all elderly and almost all from Florida.

But Bob and Sarah, who open the hotel the second week in June and close it Labor Day (they reopen without meals for the leaf season in October), started allowing children and have been attracting some younger families from the Piedmont of the Carolinas, as well as from other areas.

But how long they'll be able to keep the hotel going is in question. Each year it falls a little deeper into disrepair.

"I tell people we keep things patched with bubblegum and gray tape," Sarah said with a laugh. "We're not sure what will happen. We're going to run it this year and we'll see about next year when it comes."

(The LaBrandts did not return to reopen Balsam Mountain Inn, but the inn was later bought by a Tennessee innkeeper, Merrily Teasley,

137

who restored the exterior and the first two floors of the interior and has plans for restoring the third floor. Thirty-four rooms have been renovated and fitted with period furnishings and new mattresses. The inn is now open year-round and meals are served three times daily to guests but only Tuesday through Sunday to those who are not staying at the inn. Since its restoration, Balsam Mountain Inn has been added to the National Historic Register.)

Trip Progress Log, Day Sixteen: 24 miles
445 total miles completed, 24 to go.

DAY SEVENTEEN

Although I was facing one of the most difficult climbs on the parkway, 2,350 feet over the next eight miles to Waterrock Knob, I knew that this would be the last day of my trip. I had only 24 miles to go, an easy day's ride, even with the hard climb ahead, now that my strength and endurance had grown.

A strange and unexpected sadness overcame me, though, as I unloaded my bike and began this final day's effort. Tomorrow, I knew, I would be back to a life far removed from the parkway's beauty, serenity and many wonders. With each passing mile, this remarkable highway had absorbed a little more of me, and now I felt so much a part of it that I was reluctant to leave it.

I unconsciously set a slower pace as I started out, and I found myself lingering a little longer at each overlook.

At the view of Mount Lyn Lowry, a 6,280-foot peak near mile post 445, I chatted with a young couple and their two young children, who were drinking lemonade and waiting for the brakes to cool on their motor home after the steep ride down from Waterrock Knob. They offered me lemonade and asked if I knew the story behind the 60-foot illuminated cross on top of Mount Lyn Lowry. Only what I had read in my parkway guide, I told them. The cross had been erected in memory of a 15-year-old girl who had died of leukemia in 1962. Her parents had put it there, and Billy Graham had come to dedicate it in 1965 when the mountain was renamed for the girl. The young couple fell silent, and as we stood finishing our lemonade and watching Woodfin Cascades tumbling down the mountainside like gushing tears, I knew that they must be thinking about their love for their own children.

As I continued on up the mountain, the wild strawberries were ripe

MOUNT LYN LOWRY: This peak is named in honor of a young girl who died of leukemia.

WATERROCK KNOB: A short hike to the top of Waterrock Knob affords a view of nine mountain ranges of the Southern Appalachians. From here, you can see into South Carolina, Georgia and Tennessee, as well as North Carolina.

along the way, just as they had been on my first difficult climb up Apple Orchard Mountain. And although this climb did not seem nearly so hard, and the heat was not nearly so great, the sweet, red strawberries were just as welcome.

I made it to the parking lot at Waterrock Knob in a little more than two hours. Linda was waiting there, and we hiked up to the knob for the 360-degree view of the main mountain ranges of the Southern Appalachians: the Great Balsams, Great Smokies, Plott Balsams, Cowees, Nantahalas, Blue Ridge, Newfounds, Blacks and Great Craggies. We could see into South Carolina, Georgia and Tennessee. Mountains rolled into mountains for as far as the eye could see in every direction. We were as deep into the Appalachians as it was possible to get, and it was a comforting feeling, nestling in the bosom on the earth.

The four-and-a-half-mile ride down to Soco Gap was all too swift, with only a few overlooks along the way to break my speed.

Linda was waiting there to take me to lunch, and we loaded up the bike and drove eight miles over a winding road into Cherokee, the only town in the Qualla Reservation of the Eastern Band of Cherokees. We ate from the sumptuous buffet at a favorite restaurant, the Teepee, sitting at a table by a big window, looking out onto the swift-flowing Oconaluftee River, where two fishermen in chest waders were casting flies into the current.

"Well," I said, "I guess I'd better get back to it."

"Don't sound so glum," Linda said. "This is supposed to be fun."

"It is," I said. "That's the problem."

The last big climb began at Soco Gap, 760 feet over three miles. I stopped for the view of Maggie Valley, a tourist town on the other side of the gap from Cherokee, and again at the view of the Plott Balsams, lingering to read an exhibit telling how a German immigrant to the area had bred the famous bear hunting hounds that bear, for lack of another word, his name. From this overlook, I could see Waterrock Knob and follow the path of the parkway all the way down to Soco Gap.

At Wolf Laurel Gap, I considered taking a nine-mile spur that leads to a campground at Heintooga Overlook in the Great Smoky Mountains National Park, but I had been there before, and even though I wanted to prolong my ride, I didn't really want to add another 18 miles to it.

I would be passing through three tunnels over the next three miles, and Linda waited for me at each. Just beyond the third and longest tunnel, I turned into the overlook at Big Witch Gap. Here lived Tskil-e-gwa, called Big Witch, a Cherokee medicine man who died in 1898 at the age of 90. Big Witch was the last Cherokee eagle killer. Eagles were held sacred by the Cherokees and could be killed only by a designated person by prescribed methods so that their feathers could be used in the most important tribal rituals.

The very last climb now awaited me, an easy one, maybe a couple of hundred feet over a half mile, and it was quickly past. Just over six miles to go now – all downhill.

As I started down, I remembered an incident that had happened days earlier at Craggy Gardens. At the top of Craggy Pinnacle, I had encountered a woman and her two young grandchildren who had made the 20-minute hike to the peak to take in the magnificent view of the rhododendron balds below. Tired from the climb, the woman had taken a break on a bench.

"Just let me rest for a minute before we start back down," she said to her granddaughters.

"Going down is always harder, whether it's stairs or whether it's mountains, isn't it Grandmother?" said the elder of the two, who was perhaps six or seven.

Ah, from the mouths of babes, I now thought. Such wisdom would have eluded me when I had begun my journey along the parkway. Then I had looked forward to the downhill runs, brief though they were.

But those feelings had not been long in changing, for I soon had realized that every downhill run cost me elevation that I had struggled dearly to gain. Danger also was at its greatest while going downhill, for on the steeper grades I could build high speeds and anything – a frightened squirrel, a toot from a car coming around a blind curve, a break in the pavement – could cause an ugly, even fatal, spill. Speed, too, could cause me to miss the little things – a tiny wild flower, an unusual insect, a darting creature – that were the main reason for touring by bicycle in the first place.

Beyond that was the realization – a cliche perhaps, but true nonetheless – that the real satisfaction lay in the struggle, the accomplishment of the climb, not in the momentary but empty thrill of the easy ride down.

That last little hill had ended far short of satisfaction, and although I knew that I should be elated that I had beaten the parkway, had accomplished my goal, I was surprisingly void of that emotion. Ahead was only the emptiness of the last, long run to the end, and there was no question that it was going to be harder going down.

As I gathered speed, my mind kept drifting back over the trip. I remembered the first day, when I had thought that my ambition might be greater than my ability and that I might never make it to the end. And the third day, the most difficult of all, when I had beaten Apple Orchard Mountain and rejoiced in the knowledge that I could go the distance.

But now, strangely, I felt no sense of victory, no urge for rejoicing, just the unsettled sadness that had dogged the whole day, born of the knowledge that it all soon would be over. I tried to push it out of mind by recalling the richer moments: the pileated woodpecker near Peaks of Otter; the two yearling deer that ran alongside me at Doughton Park; the hummingbird that came so close near Mt. Mitchell, the golden foggy sunrise over the Craggies, the groundhogs that had stood on their haunches by the roadside watching me curiously all along the way; the profusion of wild flowers I had enjoyed every day, especially the flame azaleas and rhododendron, the showiest of the parkway's blossoms.

I stopped at every overlook on the way down, drinking in the last drops of this replenishing scenery, hoping to hoard enough of its spiritual nourishment to last me through the coming days when I would find myself missing it desperately. But I knew that I was only delaying the inevitable, and after pausing long at the last overlook into Big Cove, an area I knew well, I let the bike roll free and fast down the final three quarters of a mile.

Linda was waiting by the side of the road to snap my photograph as I passed the last mile post and crossed the bridge over the Oconaluftee River at the entrance to the Great Smoky Mountains National Park,

"Congratulations," she said with a smile and a kiss, when I had doubled back over the bridge to the car. "I knew you'd make it. How do you feel?"

"Like I'd like to turn around and ride it back the other way," I said.

THE FINISH: After bicycling the 470 miles of the Blue Ridge Parkway in 17 days, Jerry Bledsoe crosses the finish line.

MAJOR UPHILLS AND ELEVATION CLIMBED

SOUTHBOUND

Milepost	Total Elevation Climbed*	MAJOR UPHILLS Mileposts	Elevation Change
0-24	2,810 ft.	0-3 4.7 - 8.5 9.2 - 10.7 18.5 - 23.0	391 ft. 1,100 ft. 322 ft. 785 ft.
24.0 - 48.0	1,742 ft.	37.4 - 38.8 42.0 - 43.9 47.0 - 48.0	229 ft. 570 ft. 177 ft.
48.0 - 63.0	250 ft.	48.0 - 49.3	228 ft.
63.0 - 76.7	3,305 ft.	63.0 - 76.7	3,305 ft.
76.7 - 96.0	1,360 ft.	89.1 - 91.6 93.1 - 95.4	569 ft. 428 ft.
96.0 - 120.4	1,657 ft.	118.1 - 120.4	462 ft.
120.4 - 144.0	3,200 ft.	127.0 - 132.5 134.0 - 134.9 136.4 - 138.2	1,400 ft. 195 ft. 275 ft.
144.0 - 168.0	2,530 ft.	150.6 - 152.1 157.0 - 157.6 164.7 - 168.0	278 ft. 200 ft. 830 ft.
168.0 - 192.0	1,745 ft.	169.5 - 170.1 176.2 - 177.0 186.6 - 188.8	260 ft. 212 ft. 360 ft.
192.0 - 216.0	2,047 ft.	195.0 - 196.2 197.6 - 198.7 200.5 - 201.5	235 ft. 210 ft. 335 fl.
216.0 - 240.0	2,530 ft.	216.6 - 217.7 231.3 - 233.1 233.7 - 235.2 235.8 - 236.9	240 ft. 550 ft. 280 ft. 365 ft.
240.0 - 264.6	2,680 ft.	240.0 - 240.8 249.0 - 249.8 251.3 - 252.8 263.6 - 264.6	170 ft. 235 ft. 300 ft. 360 ft.
264.6 - 288.0	3,160 ft.	265.2 - 266.8 269.8 - 271.1 271.4 - 273.1 276.4 - 277.4 281.7 - 282.4 282.7 - 283.8 286.0 - 287.8	270 ft. 330 ft. 575 ft. 375 ft. 280 ft. 255 ft. 500 ft.
288.0 - 312.0	2,210 ft.	288.7 - 289.9 291.8 - 293.8 298.6 - 302.1	250 ft. 400 ft. 1,005 ft.
312.0 - 336.3	2,705 ft.	316.4 - 318.2 318.5 - 320.7 330.9 - 332.1 332.6 - 334.5	380 ft. 590 ft. 410 ft. 545 ft.
336.3 - 358.5	4,060 ft.	336.3 - 338.9 345 4 - 349.9 351.9 - 355.0 355.4 - 358.5	540 ft. 1,480 ft. 920 ft. 520 ft.
358.5 - 384.0	680 ft.	361.1 - 364.1	500 ft.
384.0 - 408.0	3,705 ft.	393.8 - 396.4 397.3 - 399.7 400.3 - 405.5 405.7 - 407.7	920 ft. 430 ft. 965 ft. 745 ft.
408.0 - 431.4 (431.4 is the Parkway's highest elevation)	2,775 ft.	416.8 - 420.2 423.2 - 424.8 426.5 - 428.2 429.0 - 431.4	1,100 ft. 230 ft. 405 ft. 600 ft.
431.4 - 469.1	3,450 ft.	443.1 - 451.2 455.7 - 458.9	2,450 ft. 810 ft.

* This figure represents the total amount of uphill climb within the given mileposts.

NORTHBOUND

Milepost	Total Elevation Climbed*	MAJOR UPHILLS Mileposts	Elevation Change
469.1-431.4	7,470 ft.	469.1 - 462.2 461.6 - 458.9 455.7 - 451.2 443.1 - 435.5 433.3 - 431.4	2,240 ft. 1,000 ft. 1,480 ft. 2,020 ft. 475 ft.
431.4 - 408.0 (431.4 is the Parkway's highest elevation)	1,835 ft.	426.5 - 424.8 423.2 - 421.6 415.6 - 413.2 411.9 - 409.6	325 ft. 250 ft. 385 ft. 400 ft.
408.0 - 384.0	850 ft.	No major uphills	
384.0 - 358.5	4,265 ft.	383.5 - 376.7 375.3 - 364.1 361.1 - 358.5	1,135 ft. 2,535 ft. 540 ft.
358.5 - 336.3	1,705 ft.	351.9 - 349.9 334.1 - 341.8 339.8 - 338.9	565 ft. 530 ft. 260 ft.
336.3 - 312.0	3,120 ft.	336.3 - 335.7 327.4 - 325.8 325.0 - 320.7 316.4 - 312.4	215 ft. 290 ft. 1,210 ft. 520 ft.
312.0 - 288.0	2,185 ft.	309.9 - 306.5 305.6 - 305.0 295.8 - 293.8 291.8 - 289.9	460 ft. 200 ft. 555 ft. 275 ft.
288.0 - 264.6	3,050 ft.	285.2 - 283.8 279.6 - 278.8 276.4 - 273.1 269.8 - 268.6 268.1 - 266.8	400 ft. 270 ft. 910 ft. 315 ft. 380 ft.
264.6 - 240.0	2,625 ft.	257.8 - 256.8 248.0 - 244.5 243.8 - 242.9 242.4 - 241.5	200 ft. 495 ft. 270 ft. 300 ft.
240.0 - 216.0	1,566 ft.	240.0 - 239.3 238.5 - 237.2 220.8 - 220.1	160 ft. 270 ft. 205 ft.
216.0 - 192.0	2,225 ft.	215.6 - 214.0 210.6 - 209.4 199.4 - 198.7	260 ft. 222 ft. 165 ft.
192.0 - 168.0	2,445 ft.	189.4 - 188.7 175.1 - 171.9 168.9 - 168.0	220 ft. 575 ft. 185 ft.
168.0 - 144.0	1,840 ft.	159.4 - 157.6 150.6 - 149.8	389 ft. 226 ft.
144.0 - 120.4	2,006 ft.	140.1 - 139.3 136.0 - 134.9 124.6 - 123.1 121.4 - 120.4	229 ft. 285 ft. 320 ft. 265 ft.
120.4 - 96.0	2,680 ft.	115.0 - 113.0 106.0 - 103.6 102.5 - 99.8	280 ft. 600 ft. 820 ft.
96.0 - 76.7	2,865 ft.	93.1 - 91.6 89.1 - 87.3 85.6 - 84.7 83.5 - 76.7	374 ft. 634 ft. 230 ft. 1,490 ft.
63.0 - 48.0	1,870 ft.	63.0 - 49.3	1,852 ft.
48.0 - 24.0	2,670 ft.	46.4 - 43.9 40.0 - 38.8 37.4 - 34.0	627 ft. 331 ft. 951 ft.
24 - 0	1,450ft.	13.7-10.7 9.2 - 8.5 4.7 - 3.0	563 ft. 222 ft. 300 ft.

* This figure represents the total amount of uphill climb within the given mileposts.

Chart reprinted courtesy of the National Park Service, U.S. Department of the Interior. Figures do not include climbs on spur roads, in campgrounds or picnic areas. Statistics courtesy of Tom DeVaughn, Troutville, Virginia.

WANT TO TRY IT?

Some rules, regulations, advice and books for those wanting to travel the Blue Ridge Parkway by bicycle.

Bicycle Regulations on the Parkway

1. Bicycle riders must comply with all applicable traffic regulations.

2. Bicycle riders shall keep well to the right-hand side of the road and shall keep the bicycle under complete control at all times.

3. Bicycles shall not be ridden abreast of one another.

4. Each bicycle must exhibit a white light or reflector visible at least 500 feet to the front and a red light or red reflector visible at least 200 feet to the rear during periods of low visibility or during the period between sundown and sunup.

5. Bicycles are permitted only on established public roads and parking areas. Bicycles may not be ridden on hiking trails.

6. Careless or reckless bicycle operation is prohibited.

7. Bicycle speed shall not exceed that which is reasonable and prudent with regard to traffic, weather, road and light conditions.

8. Bicycle riders shall maintain such control as may be necessary to avoid danger to persons or property.

Advice for Bicyclists on the Parkway

1. Wear a bicycle helmet.

2. Be sure your bicycle is in good repair and operating condition. Carry an air pump, spare tire and tools for minor repairs.

3. Avoid the parkway during periods of low visibility. Due to extremes in elevation, fog and rain may occur unpredictably.

4. Exercise extreme caution when riding through any of the parkway's 26 tunnels.

5. Be watchful for motorists who may not see you. A bicycle rider is far less visible than another car.

6. Bicyclists should contact a ranger prior to leaving a motor vehicle parked overnight on the parkway.

7. Due to extremes in elevation, temperatures may vary greatly. Be sure your clothing is adequate.

8. To prevent possible illness, treat any water you drink from streams and springs. Safe public water systems are available at picnic grounds and campgrounds.

9. Watch for loose gravel, rocks and branches on the parkway.

10. Camping is permitted only at established campgrounds.

11. Make an honest evaluation of your physical condition and abilities before beginning a bicycle trip on the parkway.

12. When bicycling in groups, adjust spacing to allow motor vehicles to pass safely.

For Further Reading

Maps, general information about the parkway, and specific information about campgrounds, trails and other facilities may be obtained by writing to:

The Blue Ridge Parkway
200 BB&T Building
Asheville, NC 28801

A newspaper about the parkway, *Parkway Milepost*, is published three times annually. It is distributed free to visitors along the parkway. Subscriptions are available from:

Parkway Milepost
PO Box 9892
Asheville, NC 28815

For reading about parkway history, *The Blue Ridge Parkway* by Harley E. Jolley (University of Tennessee Press) is recommended.

No parkway visitor should be without *Blue Ridge Parkway Guide* (Eastern Acorn Press), two books, dividing the parkway north and south that have been in print for more than 30 years. They were written by William G. Lord, a former parkway naturalist who later became a veterinarian, and they are as entertaining as they are informative. Lord not only lists all the sights to be seen, he details the flora and fauna, relates brief histories of specific spots and tells wonderful stories about people who once lived in the areas through which the parkway passes.